THE

EPOCH OF CREATION.

THE SCRIPTURE DOCTRINE

CONTRASTED WITH

THE GEOLOGICAL THEORY.

BY

ELEAZAR LORD.

WITH AN INTRODUCTION,

BY

RICHARD W. DICKINSON, D.D.

NEW YORK:

CHARLES SCRIBNER, 145 NASSAU STREET.

1851.

C. W. BENEDICT
Stereotyper and Printer
201 William Street.

INTRODUCTION.

WHATEVER diversity of view might be supposed to exist in relation to the divine origin of the Scriptures, it cannot be denied that they have exerted a mighty influence over the human mind, in awakening its energies and directing its inquiries. Simply to ascertain the meaning of this book, we call the *Bible*, and to set forth the high authority of its claims on the belief of all men, how many languages have been mastered, philosophies investigated, histories studied, and regions explored. Difficulties of interpretation have but served as incentives to higher mental attainments, while skeptical objections have only impelled to deeper and more varied researches, until at last, it may be said, that every department of human learning has been rendered tributary to the illustration and defence of revealed truth. We need not institute any invidious comparisons between the champions and the assailants of revelation; much less challenge its enemies to meet its friends on the fair field of open controversy. Now and then, some one, mistaking his prejudices for convictions, may talk loudly or scribble boastingly, in the hope of securing a little notoriety to his name; but they who are well read in the controversies which Christianity has occasioned, will be slow to advance objections which have been so often answered or to resort to sophistry which has been repeatedly exposed; and still more backward to employ missiles which may be so easily turned to their own discomfiture. Such, too, is the lodgment which Christianity has gained in the public mind, so deep and wide-spread the conviction that it is inseparable from the best interests of society—allied, as it is, with the purest characters, the safest counsels, the truest confidences, and the dearest charities—that whoever shall publicly aim to undermine its authority, and paralyze its influence, must necessarily labor under a disadvantage. Hence, infidelity at the present day changes its forms only that it may the more effectually conceal its designs. Now assuming some new phase of philosophy, and then intercepting our view by stratified rocks and fossil remains; now blazoning the wonders of mesmerism, or the discoveries of phrenology, and then wrapping itself in mystery, or lying encoiled in the bosom of a myth. But being less open, it may be only the more insidious, or if less virulent, it is only the more dangerous; and especially to those who, in order to keep pace with what is called "the spirit of the age," would acquaint themselves with any and every publication, though its only claim to notice may be that it is the latest issue. Works which would shock the moral sense of the community, and outrage every pious sentiment, are not to be dreaded; the infamy of such writings would counteract their malignity. The danger is, not that revelation will be rudely assailed, and overcome by invective and satire; but that it will be betrayed by a kiss; that even its professed adherents, mistaking theories for arguments, and assumptions for facts, may, in some important particulars, waive its fair and obvious meaning to save its credit with the *demi-savants* of the age.

The fact that God has made a revelation of his mind and will to man, may not be openly denied; but while his Word is admitted and professedly respected, theories are broached at variance with its doctrines, or even irreconcileable with its origin; and which, being associated with all that currently passes for philosophy and science, are, therefore, only the more imposing to those who would be held in repute for their mental independence and enlargement. Minds of this class are always the first to be captivated by anything which has the aspect of being a new view; and hence, should infidel sentiments ever obtain in the community, it will be chiefly through their influence.

Let it be considered, then, that whatever tends either to pervert or to modify the doctrines of the Gospel, is false to Christ; and in like manner, whatever tends to insinuate doubt as to the truthfulness of any portion of the Pentateuch, is false to Moses—though anything at variance with the obvious teachings of either the New or the Old Testament, must re-act to the disparagement of the other. The one necessarily involves the other; so that if the inspiration of the Gospel be admitted, that of the Pentateuch cannot be consistently denied; or if the inspiration of the latter be abandoned, that of the former cannot be proved. This is understood by the opponents of the Bible; though many who admit the great truths of the Gospel, seem to imagine that because Judaism has been abrogated, it matters not in what sense we regard the teachings of Moses: they are of no practical moment to us as Christians, and certainly need constitute no limits to the speculations of the human mind.

In some instances, we are willing to admit, that the lovers of science have not been aware of the tendency of their own views; they have been misled by the spirit of theorizing, or through a desire to make to themselves a distinctive name by deviating from received hypotheses; but in other instances, objections to the Mosaic record have been stated in so plausible a manner, that even some who hold to its credibility have been inclined to force its clear and admitted import into harmony with the positions of a Babbage or a Maillet. But if we are to reconcile the theories of geologists with the teachings of Moses, we endanger the record as effectually as we should the Gospel itself, by attempting to harmonize its doctrines with the pre-conceptions of the carnal mind; nor could there be an end to such a process, until we found ourselves hand in hand with the enemies of revelation, in demolishing its divine authority. No; let us meet all objections fairly put—whenever an answer is practicable; but when it is not—it is *legitimate* to fall back on the authority of the Bible. Here is our vantage ground: all arguments against the Bible can never outweigh the arguments in its favor.

We may be sure that nothing short of a revelation could be accompanied by such an array of proofs; but we can never be sure that all objections against the Bible do not arise from either the limited nature of our faculties, the perversion of reason, or a misapprehension of the facts in any given case. Certain it is, that no theory can adduce a moiety of the evidence which goes to establish the authenticity and genuineness of the Holy Scriptures. Reason and revelation are traceable to the same high source. Science proper cannot be divorced from religion. God's works cannot contradict his Word: hence the presumption that any conclusion from a survey of his works which clashes with the intimations of his Word, is untenable, and will yet yield to some more impartial or profound analysis of physical phenomena. Objections to the Mosaic record may be raised on divers grounds; and if we accommodate its sense to one, why not to another, and still another? If we are at liberty to abandon the cosmogony of the Pentateuch, why not, also, the fall of man, the unity of the race, the origin of animal sacrifices, and the universality of the Deluge,—until the whole record is marred by the inroads of neology, or sunk in the excavations of geology.

But whatever the form of such objections or under whatever names they are advanced, they all have the same tendency, and that is, to invalidate the inspiration and authority of the Pentateuch; and hence, in relation to the subject to which our introduction has especial reference, we are reduced to this alternative: whether to believe Moses, or to adopt the generalizations of some "hammer-bearing philosopher?"

But which should be the more competent to instruct us—a man whom God had raised up, and inspired to be the historian of creation, or one who relies on his own limited and superficial understanding as to what the Creator of the ends of the earth has or has not done? Which merits the readier credence—a record which has more historical and moral testimony in its support than any other in the world; or a science which as yet has led only a few scattered individuals to collect, as one of the most prominent among them has admitted, "some materials for future generalizations?"—a record which preserves the same lucid distinctness and commanding unity through a period of four thousand years; or a science which is but of yesterday's growth, and embraces almost as many different theories, and leads to almost as many different conclusions, as the number of its teachers?—a cosmogony, which, being in keeping with the sublime idea of creative energy, implies the *supernatural;* or one, which having originated in an induction from supposed existing causes, excludes, and stigmatizes as unscientific, all that is miraculous in the works as well as in the Word of the Creator?

We admit that, in some of our modern treatises on geology, there is much that is imposing and even fascinating to the imagination, because it borders on the nature of new discoveries; nor do we presume to deny the facts from which sage inferences are deduced; but where is the *proof* that geology has as yet legitimately accounted for the former changes on the earth's surface, much less for the time and manner of its origin? Where is the *consistency* of geological theories? What is the theory of any one writer on the subject, but the construction which he has seen fit to put on the physical phenomena of the globe, as being the exclusive effects, in his view, of the ordinary operation of natural causes? If Smith may conflict in his geological views with Buckland, and Lyell with Lamarck; or if the author of the "Footprints" may oppose the development theory of the author of the "Vestiges," with what propriety, we ask, can either demand that we shall substitute *his* understanding of the Mosaic record of the creation in the place of our own, or forfeit the respect of *scientific* men.

If geologists may draw different conclusions from the changes in the organic and the inorganic world which are now in progress, by what law of evidence are we bound either to harmonize the Mosaic record with their conflicting theories, or to discard its authority?

The work of creation was necessarily a supernatural work; and hence, all reasoning from the general laws of nature, which in their operation were subsequent to the work of creation, is as irrelevant in explanation of the Mosaic account, as the argument drawn from universal experience in disparagement of the miracles recorded in Holy Writ. Be it so, that great changes have for thousands of years been going on in the organic texture of the globe, this does not legitimate the inference that the world, when created, was not in a perfect state—having the great distinctive features of land and water, and adapted to the immediate and most exuberant production of plants and animals; and though we may see in what way soils are formed, and by what action rocks are worn away, and how what is now land may have once been a lake or the ocean, still, it does not follow that the act of creation was any less a miracle; nor that those wonderful stratified formations on which so much stress has been laid in support of certain theories, were not the result of causes acting with a rapidity and a force, of which, with all our boasted knowledge of natural philosophy and chemistry, we can form no adequate conception. To admit the original act of creation, and to attempt to account for it on natural principles, or to prescribe the mode in which the primeval creation was effected, is preposterous in the extreme; and he who so far presumes, only exposes himself to the pertinent rebuke: "Where wast thou when I laid the foundations of the earth? declare if thou hast understanding. Who hath laid the measure thereof if thou knowest; or who hath stretched out the line upon it? Whereupon are the foundations thereof fastened; or who hath laid the corner-stone thereof?"

It is of the nature of science to be governed by known laws; but it does not follow from our knowledge of natural causes that there is no supernatural agency. No; let natural science not overstep its legitimate limits, nor venture to trench on the science of Heaven's revealed will; a science, which, though it can adduce only historical and moral evidence in its support, is, by the very nature of evidence, entitled to equal weight with any mathematical demonstration. We yield to no one in our conviction of the value of scientific researches and discoveries; nor are we backward in our endeavors to resolve whatever is only seemingly miraculous into natural causes, or to explain effects if possible, on philosophical principles; but to our mind, the natural implies the supernatural, as certainly as the existence of the creature that of the Creator.

Now, to suppose, from an observation of natural causes and effects, that the world could not have been created and finished "in the space of six days and all very good," is as conclusive as to infer that man was not created in one day, because years are necessary to the maturity of the infant, or that the trees were not, because it requires a long period of time to develope the acorn. Aside from this, however, to attempt to decide the epoch of creation by science, seems to us to betray as profound ignorance of the principles of evidence, as if one should endeavor to explain the origin of Christianity by mathematics. The question respecting the origin and epoch of the creation, is not a scientific, it is simply an historical question; to be decided as we would ascertain the correctness of any other point appertaining to the department of history. If the world is older than the Mosaic account intimates, we may expect to find among the antediluvians and in the earliest state of society of which we have any knowlege, some indications of a higher antiquity; but if none are to be found—if, on the contrary, all our researches into the early condition of society only go to show that the beginning of the world we inhabit cannot be reasonably referred to a more remote period than that assigned by Moses, while his account is supported by the most exact chronological computations drawn from well-known and indisputable historical facts, then, all that remains for us, is to receive the testimony of Moses, or to reject it; and, in the latter case, to reject it simply on the ground that it is so defective as to be unworthy of reasonable credence. Science has no logical connection with the point at issue. It cannot disprove what it is not competent to establish. If it be received, it must be, not on the ground of any scientific deductions, but solely on the ground of testimony; and hence it is a point not to be either overthrown or even supported by the natural sciences; but to be believed on the credit of revelation. "By *faith*, we understand, the worlds were framed by the word of God." In all our reasonings, this great fact, that in the beginning God created and completed the heaven and the earth in the space of six days, is to be regarded as a starting point, like a first truth in philosophy, or an axiom in geometry.

He, therefore, who so far transcends the legitimate object of all true science, as to deny or even to exclude the supernatural, must needs take unwarrantable liberties with the word of God, and expose himself to the charge, if not of downright infidelity, at least of rash conjecture, extravagant fancies, and marvellous credulity. Nothing may be further from the intentions of our geologists than to afford material for sceptical thoughts; some of them profess to believe in Divine revelation; but no one can surrender his mind to the spirit of theorizing without becoming as unsafe a guide in all matters pertaining to philosophy and faith, as the partisan of any cause is, in matters of conscience and good morals. It is the judgment, rather than the integrity of those who, par eminence, claim to be the scientific guardians of the Bible, that we are constrained to doubt; nor can we welcome their aid in support of the Mosaic record, if we must accommodate its sense to the theories which they, in turn, may be induced to advance or to follow.

A firm, cordial belief in God's revelation to man, limits, while it awakens the spirit of philosophic inquiry; and had its study been pursued in connection with physical researches, its advocates would have been spared the pains of combating many a theory which leads, by necessary inference, to its rejection. We are not exciting a groundless apprehension; much less do we betray a state of mind in unison with such prejudices as were arrayed against Gallileo. To confound the advocates of the Mosaic record with the ignorant, bigoted, and persecuting priests of a dark age, is, to say the least, not very consistent with well-grounded claims to superior acumen. The discoveries of that much-injured astronomer did not conflict with revelation; but some of our modern geological theories clash directly with the teachings of Moses. Even to refer the period designated by "the beginning" to millions of ages back, in order to account for certain stratified formations and fossil remains, is to contradict the record which refers the creation of those vegetable substances of which beds of coal are composed, and of those animals of which fossils are discovered, to the third, fifth, and sixth days; or that the lights of heaven existed long before the Mosaic era, and that they then, owing to further purification of the atmosphere, on the fourth day became visible in the firmament and assumed new relations to the newly modified earth, is a supposition which cannot be reconciled with the declaration that God made two great lights, and then set them in the firmament. Hence, among the supporters of such thories may be found those who assume the ground that their faith in revelation has no connection with their views of the work of creation; who abandon not only the Mosaic account of the creation, but the unity of the race, the universality of the Deluge, and the reason for the institution of the Sabbath. Among this class, too, may be found those who discard the scriptural belief that death was the consequence of sin, and that animal sacrifices were of divine appointment; and who are wont to disparage the credibility of the miraculous portions of the Old Testament, on the ground that all the early nations were extremely prone to hyperbolize! Through the tendency of neological views on the one hand, and of geological speculations on the other, it has become not uncommon to represent the Pentateuch as a collection of popular traditions, having scarcely any more foundation in fact than the legends of classical antiquity; and, with the writings of Herodotus or the poems of Homer, to be philosophically referred to an age of fabulous uncertainty. Sometimes ridicule is employed; then difficulties are insinuated under the mask of philosophy or of science; and then again, to quiet all apprehensions, we are gravely told that the Bible is not a revelation of science! or that it can be readily explained in accordance with geological deductions by putting a different construction on this or that part, or by resolving the particulars of the Mosaic account into general terms or figurative language. But thus it is, that, through the medium of the Pentateuch, a blow is often struck at Christianity itself. We are not deceived; it will be found on inquiry, that they who attach no importance to the Mosaic account in order to secure belief in their own theories repecting the work of creation, are inclined to trace the Mosaic enactments to the prior customs of the Egyptians, and, in some instances, have no faith in the inspiration of the Old Testament.

Let us then thrust the Mosaic record aside, and what have we gained? Does it relieve our laboring minds to be able to read that, at a period too remote to be measured even by the power of imagination, God created the primordial elements? and that, after an almost boundless interval of time, he undertook what is called "the work of the first day," and which took him a thousand years to finish? Does the fond notion of myriads of ages having been employed to render this earth a fit habitation for man, relieve us from the necessity of admitting some supernatural agency in the beginning, or render any more comprehensible the time and the mode of creative energy in its material manifestations? Does it exalt our conceptions of the great God to think, that after experimenting through countless ages, at the expense of successive dynasties of beasts and reptiles, he found himself under the necessity of reducing all his work again to chaos, and of doing it all over to adapt its condition, and attemper its climate to the reasoning brain of the last product of his skill? Or, are we more deeply impressed with a sense of his greatness and glory, when, by availing ourselves of the kindly proffered aids of geology and chemistry, we have contrived to exclude all moral ends in the work of creation—thus reducing the intelligent immaterial Creator into a necessary mechanical principle of motion, groping its way through illimitable space, and at last working itself up, by chemical affinities, into outward shapes and things?

For ourselves, the Chaldean cosmogony, in which the monster Omoroca fell subdued beneath the victorious arm of the god Belus, and the world was formed out of her substance; the Hindoo, in which the Divine idea deposited in the waters, first with a thought created, a productive seed which became an egg, and in which Brahma sat inactive a whole year of the Creator; the Egyptian, which derives the visible universe from an eternal darkness in a boundless abyss; the Epicurean, which ascribes all things to a fortuitous concourse of atoms; or the Cartesian vortical theory, which teaches that a formative circular motion was originally impressed on the elements of matter,—seems to us not more unworthy of him whom we call *God* than some of the theories of modern geology, and certainly quite as *worthy* of displacing the Mosaic record in our belief.

It is by a comparison of all the pagan cosmogonies with that of Moses, that we come to give our judgment in favor of his account of the work of creation, as being the most simple, connected, and intelligible,—in every respect free from those wild and distorted images or most fanciful conceits, which form the characteristics of all ancient mythology; and in like manner, it is by looking into our modern cosmogonies, and discovering their bold assumptions, illogical generalizations, and, above all, their flagrant want of consistency, that we are led to prize the more highly the Genesis of Moses.

How unlike the god of modern science is that great Being whose account of his creative work his servant Moses was commanded to transmit to all coming ages! How presumptuous to divine his unsearchable ways by the experiments of the chemist or the classifications of the geologist! How preposterous to limit his creative energy by those aqueous and igneous agents, and those destroying, transporting, and reproductive agents which some self-complacent theorist boasts of having discovered, and thinks he understands! How impossible for the finite mind to rise to an adequate conception of his power—

> "Whose word leaped forth at once to its effect;
> Who called for things that were not, and they came!"

Because man, with his wondrous knowledge of chemical agents and mechanical forces, of sedimentary deposits and fossil remains, concludes that the Creator of the ends of the earth must have proceeded in a particular way and taken a great length of time to finish his work, does it follow that his conclusion is not a mere presumptuous conjecture? No; "ye do err, not knowing the Scriptures, nor the power of God." "His thoughts are not as our thoughts, nor his ways as our ways." The mysteries of his works are as far above our conceptions as the mysteries of his nature.

So far as we can understand his agency, God accomplishes his ends by the simplest and most direct means:—

> "In human works, though labored on with pain
> A thousand movements scarce one purpose gain;
> In God's, one single can its end produce,
> Yet serves to second too, some other use."

We delight to contemplate him as seen every where in the works of his hands; to look out on the ever-varying brilliancy and grandeur of the landscape; to gaze on the towering rocks, and the cloud-capped mountains, and the wide-spread ocean, or to look up to the magnificence of worlds on worlds which stud the firmament like gems of light, and amid all these phenomena to see the evidences of an agent which, though invisible to us, is adequate to the production of all the physical wonders by which we are surrounded. Natural science, with all its philosophical apparatus and boasted generalizations, can only secure to me a more extended vision, or a more thorough scrutiny; but it cannot inspire me with more adoring conceptions of the great First Cause of all things than a few simple expressions that may be gathered from the inspired record of God's creation. It may conduct me to distant worlds, or carry me into the dark and cavernous recesses of nature; it may point me to the inscriptions on the rocks, or to the teachings of long-buried organisms; but it can offer nothing, do nothing, to impress me with so profound a sense of the inscrutable greatness and majesty of the Divine Being—as a poor Hebrew, the son of a bondwoman, has done, by the sublime manner in which he has announced the work of creation: "In the beginning God created the heaven and the earth:"—a declaration which carries its own heaven-born evidence with it, flashing like a ray of light across the darkness of the unassisted mind, whenever it *feels after God.* Nor less impressive are the succeeding announcements: And God said, *Let there be light and there was light: Let there be a firmament*, and there was a firmament: *Let the waters under the heaven be gathered together unto one place, and let the dry land appear, and it was so.* No representation of power can be compared with this; nor has the sublimity of the narration been equalled, much less surpassed, by any subsequent writer.

He who "spake and it was done, who commanded and it stood fast," could have created the world in a moment of time; but such an act would have been altogether incomprehensible even to those created intelligences who were witnesses of his works, and who could not then, as they did when the heavens and earth were finished, "have sung together and shouted for joy." Nor could the historian have added anything to the first verse of Genesisin, explanation of an instantaneous work of such magnitude; while the bare affirmation of its having been instantly performed, though thus imparting to us the knowledge of a fact which the unassisted mind might have vainly essayed to excogitate, would have afforded but little satisfaction.

But while the narrative conveys to us this stupendous idea of an uncreated omnipotent will, it furnishes us with an account of the work of creation which is at once comprehensible, instructive, and deeply impressive. It does in no wise gratify a wanton curiosity, nor deviate from the line of its immediate object; it simply imparts to us views of God worthy of himself as the Creator, and views of man in his relations to God, of the last importance to him in furthering the great end of his being; and thus preserving brevity with simplicity, and consistency with strength, while uniting the grandest conceptions with all the sober dignity of the weightiest truths, it stands like the work which it depicts, a mighty and imperishable monument to the glory of God the CREATOR, to be seen and read by all his rational and intelligent creatures.

As it must definitively settle the point that the world was *created*, so does it furnish us with the only infallible guide in our endeavors to ascertain the manner in which the work of creation advanced.

We may reason from effects to causes, and from present to former changes on the earth's surface; but the laws of nature, (if we leave out of view their suspension or counteraction during the time of the Noachic deluge,) can guide us no farther back than to the period when God completed his work of creation; because, up to that period, be it when it might, the work was conformable to no analogy, but carried on in a manner wholly miraculous. What a work!—to create such a world as this; to fit it up with such magnificent furniture and varied conveniences; to decorate it with such ever-varied scenes of beauty and grandeur; to stock it with plants, and animals, and birds, and creeping things; to place at its head a being full formed after the image of his

Maker—all alike, and in their order, prepared for their appropriate offices, through successive seasons, from age to age. What a Mind! containing in itself the archetypes of all the forms, both of animate and inanimate things, which it called into existence by the Word of his power, without either confusion or mistake—comprehending all the parts of his creation, whether great or small—discerning all the qualities and uses of each and every object, whether separate or in combination—determining on the nature, proportions, and action of the elements, and on the operations and movements of all created existences, without deviation or hindrance, so long as the earth revolved on its axis, or the sun gladdened it with his genial rays! And what a day that, on which God, the Almighty Maker of heaven and earth, rested from his six days' work of creation! He who had performed such a work, has rights which may not be impugned, and purposes which cannot be frustrated—is infinitely worthy to be exalted to the throne of the Universe and to be held in everlasting remembrance by all his creatures; and to answer these great ends, the SABBATH was infixed in the order of Creation, and the reason for its institution reiterated in the hearing of successive generations, as often as God's commandments to mankind were repeated: "For in six days the Lord made heaven and earth, the sea and all that in them is, and rested the seventh day—wherefore the Lord blessed the Sabbath-day and hallowed it." Yes; God had higher ends in his work of creation than to furnish materials to men in after ages to theorize as to the manner in which the work advanced, or the time in which it was completed. This act asserts and attests at once his existence and his rights as the sovereign Ruler and Judge of all the earth ; it proclaims him to be, as He is, the providential and moral governor of the world, and bespeaks for him the homage and obedience of all his rational creatures: it was the manifestation of his eternal power and Godhead for purposes which the finite mind cannot fully comprehend—the initial step in the boundless range of his operations for the glory of his own incommunicable Name, and the ultimate and perfect good of all the virtuous intelligences of his vast empire!

It follows then, (and we write it with all due solemnity,) that whatever militates against the inspired record of the work of creation, cannot be regarded as harmless theory. It is treason in God's world against God's moral government; leading to a denial of his rights and to the rejection of his Word. We cannot maintain our high allegiance, and embrace any theory which would rob him of the glory due to his name ; nor can any theory be true in explanation of his works, which is opposed by the teachings, and at variance with the authority of his Word.

Such being our views, we have consented, at the request of our respected author, to express them in the form of this introduction to his work. His pages may have few attractions for those who have been fascinated by the romances of geology; and his arguments may fail to convince the advocates of modern theories—especially the few who have so laboriously aimed to enlighten the Christian public, and impose a new version of the Mosaic account. "I have written a book," said a famous theorist, "and therefore I cannot change;" and something of the kind may prejudice the judgment of many a geologist in relation to our author's work: nor may it repress that spirit of theorizing which knows no restraint from deference to revealed religion; but its perusal, we trust, will serve to relieve the minds of such as have become embarrassed by the astounding assumptions of some geological writers, and to disarm the force of gratuitous theories over those who have had but little acquaintance with the subject in its true aspects and relations.

Our author has brought to his task a mind well-stored by reading, and highly disciplined by habits of patient and independent thought. In some respects, therefore, the arguments which he employs are new, and presented in a very forcible manner; while the difficulties to which the more recent geological theories are liable in his view, at last become so obvious to the reflecting reader as to prepare him to follow the author, and with him to account, on Scriptural principles, for those phenomena which have misled certain scientific men; and to regard the Scriptural explanation of geological facts as liable to fewer objections than the most plausible theory which has yet been broached in the cabinet of the geologist, or the laboratory of the chemist. Even should the author's reasoning, in some of its points, not satisfy every reader, nor afford him all the light he may desire ; still, he will at least pause, before he succumbs to the dogmatism of a Smith, or yields his judgment to the poetic imaginings of a Miller.

That an adherence to the Mosaic account of the creation, however, will not obviate every difficulty which may be proposed, is quite certain ; that we may be unable to explain some of the phenomena to which geology points, is not improbable; but such considerations afford no more valid grounds for departing from the teachings of the Bible in relation to the work of creation, than for rejecting any one of the great doctrines which it has revealed to our faith.

Things hard to be understood by the finite mind will be found in the works as well as in the Word of an infinitely wise and all powerful Being; and with as much propriety might we reject his revelation because of physical evils which we cannot reconcile with our abstract notions of the Divine holiness and goodness, as because its account of creation does not accord with the conclusions which some geologists have "felt constrained" to adopt.

In view, then, of the sceptical tendency of certain works on the subject of geology, and more particularly the fact, that some of the professed friends of the Bible, taking for granted the assumptions of geologists, have made admissions fatal to the obvious drift and integrity of the Mosaic record, we deem it a privilege to be able to announce to the Christian public "A Treatise on the Epoch of Creation," which, while disclosing no ordinary acquaintance with scientific inquiries, is true to the Word of God. What do the Scriptures teach respecting the work of creation? is the one great question considered in this treatise. It brings to the support of the Mosaic record, arguments drawn from the laws of Biblical interpretation in relation to the use of the term, *beginning;* from the positive statement of the sacred historian, that in the space of six days the generations of the heaven and earth were completed; from the fact that throughout the Scriptures, the formation of man is referred to the same period, or included in the six days' work of creation; from the reason assigned for the institution of the Sabbath, and for the *stress* afterwards laid on this fact, growing out of the antagonism of all idolatrous systems of religion to the acknowledgment of God's rights as the Creator; from the fact that the delegated work of Christ is referred to the same period with the creation, and from the glory and honor due and ascribed to *Him,* "without whom was not anything made that was made."

Such are the author's main positions; and if they

are untenable, then the Sabbath can no longer be regarded as the divine memorial of God's six days' work of creation: we must be governed in all our inquiries on the subject of creation by our knowledge of physical laws, not by God's written Word; and, surrendering our minds to the "principles of geology," we are left, not only to doubt the truthfulness of the Mosaic record of the creation, but to incline to the opinion that matter itself is eternal!

R. W. D.

NEW YORK, *July* 7, 1851.

CONTENTS.

CHAPTER IV.

CHAPTER V.

CHAPTER VI.

CHAPTER VII.

CHAPTER VIII.

CHAPTER IX.

CHAPTER X.

THE EPOCH OF CREATION.

CHAPTER I.

Observations relating to the Subject of Inquiry—The Main Question not Involved in the Facts or Inductions of Geological Science—Relation of it to the Scriptures.

THE geological theory assigns to the physical world a far higher antiquity than it allows to the human race. Many who believe in the inspiration of the Scriptures, adopt this theory, to avoid the difficulties which geological science is supposed to present to the doctrine which ascribes the creation of man and that of the earth to one and the same epoch; and they endeavor so to construe the language of Scripture as to make it harmonize with what they suppose to be the unavoidable conclusions of science. If they regard the Scriptures with the reverence due to them, they must yield to the required interpretations, under the impression that the credit of revelation itself demands them, that they affect no essential doctrine, that the alleged conclusions of science can in no other way be met, and that this course may conciliate and win the confidence and faith of scientific men, who otherwise would be in danger of rejecting the Bible altogether.

In pursuing this course, however, in relation to the epoch of creation, they make concessions in construing the language of Scripture, which, if made in construing that language on other scriptural subjects, may lead to the subversion of every statement and doctrine by which the Bible is distinguished as a revelation from God. They seem, on the one hand, to forget that the laws of language are as fixed and as intelligible as those of any science; and on the other, that the geologist, in his inquiries, is restricted to physical phenomena as seen under the operation of physical causes, or natural laws, to the exclusion of every thing supernatural. The phenomena of his science are therefore studied with sole reference to those natural causes which are operating to produce the observed or analogous results. To admit the present or past operation of a supernatural cause, would be to surpass the bounds of physical enquiry. Thus in studying the sedimentary formations which constitute perhaps three quarters of the solid surface of the globe, the geologist discovers that there are in operation natural causes which are gradually producing somewhat similar deposits. Those causes only fall within his observation. They are the appropriate natural causes of such effects; and if allowed to have been in operation long enough, are supposed adequate to have produced the results in question. If, as a scientific geologist, he ascribes the facts which he discovers to a supernatural cause—a cause not within his observation—he passes out of his own field of inquiry into that of revelation; out of the province of science into that of theology. His business is with physical phenomena, which come directly within his own observation; with facts, and their relations and connections. It does not invade, and has nothing to do with, other departments of knowledge. If any supernatural cause has been at any period, or for any reason, interposed, to produce the facts which he observes; if any miracle has been wrought, the consideration of it is not within his province. It belongs to a different department. He waives the subject as inappropriate to him, and out of his sphere. Whether miracles are possible, whether there has ever been a necessity or sufficient reason for them, or whether they have ever actually been interposed, it is not his object to enquire. It is the business of the physical science which he pursues, to account for all the facts observed on natural principles, and by means of ordinary physical laws. If they can be so accounted for, the occurrence of miracles in their production ought not to be supposed. To suppose them would be unscientific and unnecessary. Great progress, it is argued, has already been made in accounting for the facts of geology in this manner; and if in some cases a satisfactory explanation has not been rendered, the defect may be reasonably ascribed to our remaining ignorance of physical causes and their operations. In view of what has been done, it may be hoped that further researches will clear up what now remains obscure. When that is accomplished, the exact truth will be scientifically established, and that of course will not conflict with the real meaning of any Divinely inspired statement.

In taking this view of the matter, the geologist proceeds upon the assumption, or conviction, that the conclusions which he has arrived at in regard, for example, to the mode in which the sedimentary formations, with their imbedded fossils, were formed, and consequently, in regard to the extreme remoteness of the era of creation, are true, and entitled to much the same confidence as mathematical demonstrations. And under such impression, he has no difficulty in concluding that the earth, in order to a sufficient lapse of time to admit of the gradual formation of the sedimentary deposits, must have been created long before the creation of man; and if it is the apparent import of the Mosaïc narrative, that they were created simultaneously in the "six days;" such, if that narrative is inspired, cannot be its real import. It must be so construed as to harmonize with the conclusions which the geologist has adopted. He thinks those conclusions so far settled, and entitled to such confidence, as to make it necessary to the believer in revelation to construe the Mosaic record in accordance with them. In other words, he deems it more likely that the apparent is not the true meaning of that record, than that any other besides natural, ordinary, physical causes have been employed to produce the sedimentary formations, or other phenomena with which his inquiries are concerned. If there is a defect anywhere, he supposes it must be in the written account of the creation, and not in his ascription of changes to the slow operation of natural causes. He supposes it to be more likely that a written account, in a dead and very ancient language, should appear to mean what it does not mean, that it should be figurative or mystical, that it should be misconstrued through ignorance, or by reason of its brevity or other peculiarities, than that he should be mistaken in his inferences from the geological phenomena of the earth. The allowance out of a past eternity, of periods of time sufficient to admit of all the observed phenomena being produced by the gradual operations of these natural causes, appears to him to be less objectionable, more scientific, and more satisfactory every way, than to suppose that supernatural causes have been interposed.

Resting in this view, he does not feel himself called

on to enquire whether the inspired record, construed by the invariable laws of language, has not higher claims, and is not of more certain import, than his inference from the facts of physical science considered as the result of the ordinary laws of nature; whether that record does not inform us of moral reasons for the creation of the earth and for great changes in its condition, and allege the occurrence, for moral reasons, of supernatural interpositions, on various occasions; whether the admission of moral, in connection with physical, reasons and causes, in all the works of creation and providence, and in the moral and physical government of the world, is not absolutely indispensable, if the Creator exercises such government; since a moral disconnected from a physical government, over creatures having physical natures and in close alliance with physical things, is undoubtedly impossible—whether, in the administration of such a government, operations which we call supernatural are any less natural to the Creator, or any less likely to be interposed when there is a moral reason, or any sufficient exigency or occasion for them, than operations which occur in conformity to what we call the laws of nature; since, in the administration of his government, the latter, as truly as the former, are employed and controlled by the Creator. Whether in the case of the changes which are disclosed by geological research, the lapse of such rounds of duration, as are supposed to have been necessary for their production, is not more improbable and incredible than that they should have been hastened by supernatural interference, especially if they are considered as having taken place under the administration and control of a Being of infinite wisdom, power, and goodness; and if, supposing such prolonged periods to have elapsed, and to have been succeeded by a new creation, including man, the comparative uselessness and nullity of the earlier changes are taken into view. Whether in accounting for the supposed gradual formation of the sedimentary rocks, the distribution in them of marine and terrestrial plants and animals, and the preservation of their most delicate forms, there may not be difficulties which no operation of the laws of nature could possibly overcome—difficulties in respect to the supply of the peculiar materials of the respective strata, the supply of relics from the land and sea together in the same rocks, and the conservation of them during the long periods required for the inhumation of each and every one of them, by the slow operation of natural causes, to overcome which would require a stupendous, universal, and constant supernatural interposition.

The argument, or inference, of the geologist in support of the high antiquity of the earth, is not in itself by any means conclusive; and the theory which it involves is obnoxious to very grave objections besides those derived from the Scripture record, and to still more formidable objections from the teachings of the sacred oracles.

The question at issue is, whether the Mosaic account of the creation is an account of the original creation out of nothing of the material worlds and all that in them is; or whether the narrative of the "six days" is an account only of the remodelling of the earth—one of those worlds—out of the materials of the same earth created at an earlier period, supposed to be indicated by the phrase "in the beginning."

This question is not of a nature to be determined by scientific discoveries or deductions. It involves considerations of which physical science is not cognizant, and does not in any way include. It involves the fact itself of a creation of the heavens and the earth. The only probable reason which geology furnishes in favor of the supposition that the earth was created, or had a beginning at any period, however remote, is, as represented by Dr. Buckland, that beneath the lowest stratum of sedimentary rocks no fossil remains of plants or animals have been discovered, and therefore it is inferred that the deposition of such fossils must have had a beginning, and thence that plants and animals themselves had a beginning. From this reasoning, though he does not formally state the inference, we seem to be expected to infer that the earth itself, as well as its plants and animals, had a beginning. "We argue thus," he says: "It is demonstrated from geology that there was a period when no organic beings had existence; these organic beings must therefore have had a beginning subsequently to that period; and where is that beginning to be found but in the will and *fiat* of an intelligent and all-wise Creator."* The demonstration, however, as he afterwards admits, relates only to those organized beings whose fossil remains are discovered. Geology neither does nor can demonstrate that there were not earlier races of organized beings than those whose fossil remains are now discovered; races indefinitely numerous, diversified, and chronologically separated, whose remains are beneath the rocks which contain the fossils of modern geology, and therefore have not been discovered; or have been destroyed by the melting up of those lower rocks, or have otherwise been obliterated by the progress of change, or have ceased to exist, under circumstances and in a condition of the earth which precluded their being fossilized. Geology, therefore, furnishes no conclusive evidence, nor, at best, anything more than a faint and doubtful probability that the earth has not existed and been occupied with plants and animals from eternity. The

* Bridgewater Treatise.

most probable inference from it, on supposition that immeasurable rounds of duration were required for the formation of the strata in which fossils are now discovered, would be that the earth had existed for ever. On this head nothing can resolve or satisfy us but a revelation from Him who created the world; and who, according to the revelation which he has made, created it as part and parcel of a system of things which included moral as well as physical agencies and ends, and which, alike under his moral and physical government, he has ever been carrying into effect. The question, like that concerning the unity of the human race, can be determined only by revelation. The two subjects belong to one and the same system of things, and are associated in the same moral purposes and government, in the progress of which the dead are to be raised, and the earth is to be renovated, not by a natural or gradual process, but by supernatural interposition.

When we learn from a venerable professor of one of our oldest Literary Institutions, that "he cares not whether the earth was created perfect, or was formed out of nebular matter, or elaborated out of primordial elements; the manner and epoch of its origin having nothing to do with his faith in the Scriptures;" and when we have it under the sanction of one of the most respected professors in one of the oldest and soundest of our theological seminaries, that "There is no need to be much concerned about the age of the globe on which our race resides. The chronology of Moses is that of the human race, and not that of the material part of the earth. All that is necessary to relieve the sacred history from every objection on this ground is to interpret the first sentence in the Bible as stating the fact, that the heavens and the earth were created by God, without stating at what time, and considering the six days' creation to relate to the preparation, and organization of the Chaotic Materialism into a form and condition to suit its new inhabitants:" we may reasonably expect it to be asked, Why should we concern ourselves about these questions? Of what consequence can it be to us, whether the earth was created infinite ages, or only 6000 years ago? The answer is, that the question very nearly concerns the supremacy and glory of the Creator, and the faith, reverence, and homage of men. He has made known the facts in a revelation in which the creation of the heavens and earth holds the first and prominent place; as being the basis of his rights and prerogatives over his creatures as their providential and moral governor; and as the initiatory step in the wide and endless range of his plan of operations and manifestations to the whole universe of intelligent agents. In this world to which that revelation was made, the question has, from the era of the apostasy, been under debate, whether the self-existent, the Jehovah of the Bible, was, indeed, the Creator of the material worlds, and all creatures; or, whether they were created by a good or an evil angel, or other creature; or whether they were eternal, and owed their successive races of organized beings, and their changes of condition, to a coeval and inherent law of development. If the worlds were created, if their existence was originated, if they were brought into being by the will of an intelligent Being, then he, as their Creator, necessarily and of right is their proprietor, lawgiver, and ruler, and unqualified homage, obedience, and praise are due to him on that account. But it is of the essence of apostasy and rebellion, to deny those prerogatives and rights, and to refuse to yield such homage and obedience; and of such denial and refusal the history of the world almost wholly consists. And if out of deference to a physical theory which, to say the least, leaves the fact of any beginning or creation of the world in extreme doubt and uncertainty, we consent so to modify the revelation which the Creator himself has made, as to sever, by incalculable periods, the creation itself from the exercise and assertion of the rights, prerogatives, and moral purposes of the Creator, as Lawgiver and Moral governor, we so far really or virtually deny those prerogatives, rights, and purposes. For we thereby invade or annul the revealed plan, which most emphatically and comprehensively includes and connects the creation of all things with that of man, and on that ground asserts the prerogatives and rights of moral government, and claims unqualified homage and obedience.

Now, since geology, while it acquaints us with innumerable facts concerning the physical condition of the earth, is wholly incompetent to explain the conditions or circumstances in which, the reasons for which, or the mode of operation by which, those facts were produced; it is necessary to have recourse to the inspired oracles as the only means of attaining any satisfaction.

The Holy Scriptures furnish us with a detailed account of the work of creation, as well as of the wondrous works of Providence and Grace. The creation of the heavens and earth, and all that in them is, being necessarily in the order of Divine manifestations and purposes, before and preliminary to the works of providence and redemption, is first narrated in the sacred oracles. The Creator himself being also the Lawgiver, Ruler, and Revealer, and the creation being the ground of his prerogatives and rights as providential and moral Governor; his revealed account of the work of creation we should expect would be not only in harmony with his other works, and with his entire scheme of operations, but in itself as intelligible as any other portion of the history of his acts. And so undoubtedly it is. It ascertains to us the fact of the creation of all things out of nothing, the order in which they were produced, and their relations and connections with his moral purposes and administrations.

This narrative apparently teaches us that the heavens and earth, and all their hosts, including man, were created at one and the same epoch—in the space of six days. The geologists infer from the facts disclosed by their researches, that the material world must have existed many myriads of ages prior to the creation of man. To reconcile the Mosaic narrative with the supposition of such earlier date, they conclude that the first verse of Genesis constitutes, unconnected with the narrative of the six days, a distinct announcement that the heaven and earth were created at an indefinitely remote period, indicated by the word "*beginning*." On this hypothesis they suppose that revelation and the geological theory concerning the creation may be consistent with each other. No other announcements of the sacred oracles are supposed by them to be in conflict with geology. The difficulty relates to the phrase, "*in the beginning*," which they suppose imports and refers to a commencement of time long anterior to the six days, as if the verse were read, In the beginning *of time* God created the heaven and the earth.

That they are mistaken in this supposition, an examination of the subject will, it is presumed, satisfactorily show. And it may appear, that believing all Scripture to have been given by inspiration of God, and that his rights and prerogatives as moral Governor are founded in the fact of his being the Creator and upholder of all things, it as truly concerns us to know what relates to the work of creation and its epoch, as to know what relates to the allegiance due to him from us, or what relates to our moral condition, the method of recovery, or the destiny which awaits us.

CHAPTER II.

The Epoch of Creation according to the Scriptures—Import of the phrase, "In the beginning"—Usage of that and analogous phrases—The Sabbath appointed to be observed as a public acknowledgment and attestation, that Jehovah created all things in the space of six days—The significance and importance of that fact in relation to the rival system of Idolatry.

THE Hebrew word, Gen. i. 1, rendered in our English version, "In the beginning," occurs eighteen times in the Books of Moses, and elsewhere thirty-two times in fourteen other books of the Old Testament. But it does not in any one of these instances denote an epoch, or any date or space of time. It is employed only to denote the head of a class, the commencement of a process, or the first of a series of things, persons, acts, or events. The evidence of this fact will demonstrate that the first verse of Genesis does not refer to a remote anterior creation of the heavens and the earth, but is as certainly as any succeeding verse of the chapter a part of the narrative of the "six days" work of creation.

In twenty-one out of the whole number of instances in which the original word occurs, it is translated "first-fruits," or first of the fruits of the land—corn, wine, &c.—in all which it is evidently restricted to the products or things then existing, or the series with which they were immediately connected. Thus:

"The first of *the first-fruits* of thy land"—*the beginning* of thy land, the products earliest ripe—"thou shalt bring into the house of the Lord thy God."—Exod. xxiii. 19, and xxiv. 26.

"When ye come into the land which I give you, and shall reap the harvest thereof, then ye shall bring a sheaf of *the first-fruits*"—*the beginning*—"of your harvest unto the priest."—Levit. xxiii. 10.

"All the best of the oil, and all the best of the wine, and of the wheat, *the first-fruits*"—*the beginning*—"of them, they shall offer unto the Lord."—Numb. xviii. 12.

"Ye shall offer up a cake of *the first*"—*the beginning*—"of your dough for a heave-offering." Of *the first*"—*the beginning*—"of your dough ye shall give unto the Lord a heave-offering."—Numb. xv. 20, 21.

"Amalek was *the first*"—*the beginning*—"of the nations."—Ibid. xxiv. 20.

"*The first*"—*the beginning*—"of the fleece of thy sheep shalt thou give him."—Deut. xviii. 4, and again xviii. 4.

"Thou shalt take of *the first*"—*the beginning*—"of all the fruit of the earth, which thou shalt bring of thy land, that the Lord thy God giveth thee."—Deut. xxvi. 2.

"I have brought *the first-fruits*,"—*the beginning*, "of the land."—Deut. xxvi. 10.

"The children of Israel brought in abundance, *the first-fruits*," *the beginning*, "of corn, wine, and oil, and honey, and of all the increase of the field."—2 Chron. xxxi. 5.

"Honor the Lord with thy substance, and with *the first-fruits*," *the beginning*, "of all thine increase."—Prov. iii. 9.

"They shall not sell of it, neither exchange, nor alienate, *the first-fruits*,"—*the beginning*—"of the land."—Ezekiel xlviii.

See also Levit. ii. 12; Nehemiah x. 37, and xii. 44; Jer. ii. 3; Ezekiel xx. 40 and 44; xxx. twice; Hosea ix. 10.

The offering of first-fruits was a duty to be performed immediately on commencing the harvest. The *first-fruits* were the first sheaves, *the beginning*, of the harvest. And as the harvest was accomplished by a continued series of operations of which the gathering of the first sheaves was *the beginning*, so the work of creation was accomplished by a series of operations during six days; of which operations the creation of the celestial bodies and the earth, was the first, *the beginning.*

In the Mosaic narrative, the fact that God *created* the heavens and the earth, the sea and all that in them is, is the chief thing asserted. But he effected the work of creation by a series of acts. *The first-fruits* of his creative energy, the first act in the series of his acts as Creator, *the beginning*, was the creation of the earth and the heavenly bodies; next light, and successively plants and trees, marine and aerial creatures, land animals, and man. Intermediately the waters were divided, the seas separated from the dry land, and the light made to radiate from the sun, moon, and stars, to illumine the revolving earth. Hence the same word which was employed to denote the first in the series of creative acts, was employed to denote the first in the series of the reaper's acts in gathering his harvest; and the first verse of Genesis would have conveyed the same meaning as now, had it read: "God created all things; the celestial orbs and the earth were the first products of his creative energy!"

This illustration of the usage and import of the word in question is confirmed by its use elsewhere. In eighteen instances it is translated "In the beginning, from the beginning," &c., where its import and reference are manifestly the same as in the passages above cited. For example:

" *The beginning* of Nimrod's kingdom was Babel." —Gen. x. 10. The building of Babel was the first proceeding, the *first-fruit*, the commencement of that series of measures by which Nimrod founded and erected a kingdom.

" Reuben, thou art my first-born, *the beginning* of my strength."—Gen. xlix. 3. Reuben was the first of twelve sons, *the first-fruit* of Jacob's strength.

" From *the beginning* of the year even unto the end of the year."—Deut. xi. 12. The beginning of a year is the first of a series of days which compose a year, and which immediately succeed each other.

" Though thy *beginning* was small, yet thy latter end should greatly increase." " The Lord blessed the latter end of Job more than his *beginning*."—Job viii. 7, and xlii. 12. " The fear of the Lord is *the beginning* of wisdom."—Psalm cxi. 10. " The fear of the Lord is the beginning of knowledge."—Prov. i. 7. " *The beginning* of strife is as when one letteth out water."—Prov. xvii. 14. " The Lord possessed me *in the beginning* of his way."—Prov. viii. 22. " Better is the end of a thing than *the beginning* thereof."—Eccl. vii. 8. " Declaring the end from *the beginning*."—Isa. xlvi. 10. " *In the beginning* of the reign of Jehoiakim."—Isa. xxvi. 1, and xxvii. 1. " *In the beginning* of the reign of Zedekiah."—Jer. xxviii. 1, and xlix. 34. " *In the beginning* God created the heavens and the earth."—Gen. i. 1. See also Deut xxi. 17; Micah i. 13.

In nine instances the same word is translated "*chief*," as *chief* of the ways of God; *chief* of the offerings; *chief* of their strength; *chief* of the nations; *chief* of the children of Ammon. And in one of the remaining cases of its occurrence it is rendered "*the first part*;" and in the other, "*the principal thing*."

Now to suppose that the act which was first in that series of acts which brought into existence the works of creation, was separated from the second act in that series by an interval of countless myriads of ages, is, so far as the invariable usage of this word determines its meaning, no less preposterous than to suppose that the gathering of the first sheaves of each annual harvest was separated from the remainder of the same harvest by a similar lapse of ages; that the building of Babel was separated by a like interval from the other proceedings of Nimrod in founding his kingdom; that the birth of Jacob's first son was in like manner separated from that of the others; that the first day of a year was separated from the ensuing days of the same year, and contemplated as immeasurably earlier in time; or that the beginning of a king's reign might mean an epoch earlier by incalculable periods than the day of his birth.

It is thus conclusively evident that Dr. Buckland,

Dr. Smith, and others, who assume that the phrase "*In the beginning*" signifies a distant epoch or point of time indefinitely earlier than the "six days," have totally mistaken or overlooked the meaning and object of the original word; it being manifest, from the usage and connection of it with the context, in every instance in which it occurs in the Old Testament Scriptures, that its import and object are not in any instance to denote, or refer to any epoch, date, or relation of time whatever. And if they are thus mistaken in regard to the meaning of that word, then the first verse of the first chapter of Genesis, equally with the verses which succeed it, is part of the narrative of the creation of all things in the space of six days; and if geology, as a science, teaches that the earth was created at an earlier epoch than man, it can neither derive any countenance from the first verse of Genesis, nor be reconciled with the narrative of the six days.

But there are in the Scriptures many other evidences to the same effect. The creation of the world and of man is often asserted or referred to in terms and connections which wholly forbid any other conclusion.

In the New Testament, the words corresponding with that which in the first of Genesis is translated "beginning," are uniformly employed in the same manner, and in like restricted connection, with the things affirmed in the immediate context. Thus:

"He which made mankind *in the beginning*, made them male and female."—Matthew xix. 4.

"*From the beginning* of the creation God made them male and female."—Mark x. 6.

"Moses suffered you to put away your wives; but from *the beginning* it was not so."—Matth. xxiv. 8.

"These are *the beginning* of sorrows."—Matth. xxiv. 8.

"*The beginning* of the Gospel."—Mark i. 1.

"In those days shall be affliction such as was not from *the beginning* of the creation, which God created unto this time."—Mark xiii. 19.

"This beginning of miracles did Jesus in Cana."—John ii. 11.

These passages, without citing others to the same effect, clearly show that the original words are used not to denote an epoch or date of time, but to distinguish the first of a class or succession of things. Mankind were created male and female at the beginning of the race—the first individuals of the race were so created. Moses allowed a practice which was not allowed at the beginning—the commencement of social relations. The first of a series of afflictions, and the first sentence written in the narrative of the

Gospel, respectively mark the commencement of a class of things, not a date or epoch in time. Affliction to be endured by a portion of the human race, exceeding any since the beginning of the creation, doubtless means that creation which comprised the heavens, the earth, and the first of such creatures as were to endure the affliction predicted. For a comparison of what they were to endure could not be made with anything that happened ages before the first of their race were created. The beginning of miracles was the first of a series of supernatural interpositions.

Thus we are again shut up to the conclusion that the narrative of the six days, in the first chapter of Genesis, includes the first verse of that chapter equally with the other verses; and that the celestial orbs and the earth were created at that, and not at an earlier epoch.

Accordingly, because God created the heavens and the earth, the sea and all that in them is, in six days, and rested the seventh day, He blessed and hallowed *that* as a day of rest for man, and enjoined on him the observance of it. His moral government being founded in his prerogatives and rights as Creator, He alleges his creation of all things in six days as the reason for his hallowing the seventh day, and requiring man to remember and keep it.

The Moral Law, announced to the Israelites from

Sinai in a voice which shook the earth, and amid the most awful signals and attestations of the presence of the Creator and Lawgiver, is as unmistakable in its meaning, as it is comprehensive and emphatic in its terms. "Remember the Sabbath day to keep it holy. Six days shalt thou labor and do all thy work, but the seventh day is the Sabbath [rest] of the Lord thy God. In it thou shalt not do any work ; thou, nor thy son, nor thy daughter, thy man-servant, nor thy maid-servant, nor thy cattle, nor the stranger that is within thy gates : FOR, *in six days the Lord made heaven and earth, the sea and all that in them is, and rested the seventh day :* WHEREFORE *the Lord blessed the Sabbath day and hallowed it.*"—Exod. xx.

So, in the rehearsal of its import, in connection with their moral obligations and the threatened penalty, on the delivery of the tables of stone, after the ritual law, and the directions concerning the tabernacle and its services had been given : "The Lord spake unto Moses, saying, Speak thou also unto the children of Israel, saying, Verily my Sabbaths ye shall keep, for it is *a sign* between me and you throughout your generations, that ye may know that I am the Lord that doth sanctify you. Ye shall keep the Sabbath therefore : for it is holy unto you. Every one that defileth it, shall surely be put to death : for whosoever doeth any work therein, that soul shall be cut off from among his people. Six days may work be done, but in the seventh, is the Sabbath of rest holy to the Lord: whosoever doeth any work in the Sabbath-day, he shall surely be put to death. Wherefore the children of Israel shall keep the Sabbath to observe the Sabbath, throughout their generations, for a perpetual covenant. It is *a sign* between me and the children of Israel forever: For in six days the Lord made heaven and earth, and on the seventh day he rested." —Exod. xxxi.

The seventh day was thus consecrated and set apart as a sign, token, commemorative attestation of the fact that in six days the Lord created the heavens and the earth, the sea and all that in them is; and that fact was so essential to the assertion and validity of his claims as Lawgiver and Ruler, that whosoever refused or omitted to acknowledge it, by refusing or omitting to observe the prescribed sign, was therefore to be put to death.

From the nature of the sign—the consecration and observance of the seventh day—it is obvious that the reason why that was appointed instead of any other significant ordinance, was, as the text so emphatically declares, because the work of creation had been accomplished in six days. That sign in preference to any other could not have been prescribed, had the heavens and earth been created myriads of ages before the creation of man.

To guard the Israelites against idolatry, and against infidelity and error as to their Creator and his prerogatives, it was of the utmost importance to institute a memorial of his works as Creator, a remembrancer, a sign, distinct from their ordinary avocations, to recur and be recognized at frequent intervals, interwoven with their religious obligations and duties, and sanctioned by a penalty as severe as that denounced upon idolaters.

The Sabbath was instituted in paradise, and no doubt was observed and regarded from that time forward as a sign, and testimony that in the six natural days which preceded its institution, the Lord created the heavens, the earth, the seas, and all that in them is, and rested on the consecrated seventh day. Hence when the manna was first dispensed in the wilderness, shortly after the passage of the Red Sea, and prior to the scenes at Sinai, we read Exod. xvi. 23, that on the sixth day the people gathered a double supply, and Moses said, " This is that which the Lord hath said, to-morrow is the rest of the holy Sabbath unto the Lord." He then directs them to use what was needful on the sixth day, and the remainder on the seventh, the Sabbath day, when there would be none in the field. " Six days shall ye gather it ; but on the seventh, which is the Sabbath day, there shall be none."

To maintain the conviction and public acknowledgment of the fact that in six days God created the heavens and earth, the sea, and all things therein, was to maintain the conviction and public acknowledgment that Jehovah the self-existent, the God of Israel, was the Creator ; and that he accomplished the work of creation, not at different, undefined, and unknown periods, but at one period, one epoch, a defined, appreciable, familiar space of six days. The idolatry (namely the worship of Bel, Baal, Beelzebub, Satan) which prevailed in Egypt and in Canaan when Moses wrote, denied these facts ; and regarded the world as eternal, or ascribed the works of creation as it did the works of providence, to the created intelligence denominated Bel, Baal, &c., and assigned to him the sun as his tabernacle and Shekina. The antagonism and rivalship of Satan required the homage of his followers ; to secure which, required on his part, the arrogation of those works, prerogatives, and rights, on which the claims of Jehovah as Creator and moral governor were founded. Hence to side with that arrogant and usurping adversary, disregarding the Divine testimony concerning the fact of the creation in six days, forgetting, despising, and violating the hallowed seventh day as the appointed sign and memorial of that fact, and thereby denying that Jehovah was the Creator, and that, because he created all things, he was entitled to their universal homage and obedience, was treason against him, and deserved the penalty of death.

In view of these considerations, the necessity, appropriateness, grandeur, and beauty, of the first table of the Decalogue is apparent. There is a striking significance in the order and succession of commands. Thou shalt have no other gods before me; in my sight, or in preference to me. Thou shalt not make, bow down to, or serve any graven image, or any likeness of anything in heaven or earth, any creature supposed to exist in the celestial orbs, or any creature on earth; for I the Lord thy God am a jealous God. Thou shalt not take the name of the Lord thy God in vain. Remember the Sabbath day to keep it holy! It is quite apparent from these inhibitions, that it was the impious rival system of idolatry that was to be resisted and avoided, as denying the Jehovah to be the Creator, and therefore the only lawgiver and ruler, and as ascribing his prerogatives to creatures.

Idolatry then, and ever since, has not only denied the exclusive claims of Jehovah to homage and obedience, but has been no less conspicuously characterized as substituting creature mediators and intercessors, in place of the one Divine Mediator. It is a rival system; a false religion in opposition to the true; a system of creature worship in opposition to the worship of God the Creator. To prohibit and guard against it, therefore, was of the highest importance. It usurped the homage and allegiance which was due to God the Creator, and stood forth in public and arrogant opposition to him, in its forms, examples, and pretensions; and therefore he regarded it with jealousy and indignation, and declared himself in relation to it, "a jealous God, a consuming fire!" "They provoked him to jealousy with strange gods, with abominations provoked they him to anger. They sacrificed unto devils, not to God; to gods whom they knew not. Of the Rock that begat thee thou art unmindful, and hast forgotten *God that formed thee.* And when the Lord saw it he abhorred them; and he said, I will hide my face from them. They have moved me to jealousy with that which is not God, they have provoked me to anger with their vanities." —Deut. xxxii. 16–21. Again; "If there should be among you man or woman, or family, or tribe, whose heart turneth away from the Lord our God, to go and serve the gods of these nations, the Lord will not spare him, but then the anger of the Lord and his jealousy shall smoke against that man, and all the curses that are written in this book shall lie upon him."—Deut. xxix. 18–20.

To show the impotence and vanity of idols it is said: "The Lord is the true God; He is the living God, and an everlasting king; at his wrath the earth shall tremble, and the nations shall not be able to abide his indignation. Thus shall ye say unto the gods *which have not made the heavens and the earth*, even they shall perish from the earth, and from under these heavens. He hath made the earth by his power; He hath established the world by his wisdom, and hath stretched out the heavens by his discretion. Every man is brutish in his knowledge; every founder is confounded by the graven image; for his molten image is falsehood, and there is no breath in them. They are vanity and the work of errors; in the time of their visitation they shall perish. The portion of Jacob is not like them; but *he is the former of all things*."—Jer. x. 10–16.

The creation and proprietorship of the heavens and the earth are often ascribed to Jehovah as the ground of his claim to supreme homage and obedience, and his prohibition of idolatry. Thus Moses in his exhortation —Deut. x. and xi. "And now, Israel, what doth the Lord thy God require of thee, but to fear the Lord thy God, to walk in all his ways, and to love him, and to serve the Lord thy God with all thy heart and with all thy soul, to keep the commandments of the Lord and his statutes, which I command thee this day for thy good. Behold the heaven, and the heaven of heavens is the Lord's thy God, the earth also, with all that therein is. Take heed to yourselves, that your heart be not deceived, and ye turn aside, and serve other gods, and worship them; and then the Lord's wrath be kindled against you, and He shut up the heavens that there be no rain, and that the land yield not her fruit, lest ye perish quickly," &c.

"By the Word of the Lord were the heavens made, and all the host of them by the breath of his mouth. He gathereth the waters of the sea together as a heap: he layeth up the depth in storehouses. Let all the earth fear the Lord. Let all the inhabitants of the world stand in awe of him. For he spake and it was done, he commanded and it stood fast."—Ps. xxxiii.

"Their idols are silver and gold, the work of men's hands; they that make them are like unto them; so is every one that trusteth in them. O Israel, trust in the Lord. Ye are blessed of the Lord which made heaven and earth."—Psalm cv.

When Sennacherib trusting in his idols invaded Judea and sent to reproach and defy the God of Israel, Hezekiah prayed, saying, "O Lord of hosts, God of Israel, that dwellest between the cherubims, thou art the God, even thou alone, of all the kingdoms of the earth: thou hast made heaven and earth."—Isa. xxxvii.

"Great is the Lord, and greatly to be praised: he also is to be feared above all gods. For all the gods of the people are idols; but the Lord made the heavens."—1 Chron. xvi.

"Thus saith God the Lord, he that created the heavens and stretched them out, he that spreadeth forth the earth, and that which cometh out of it, I am the Lord, that is my name; and my glory will I not give to another, neither my praise to graven images." —Isa. xlii.

"They that make a graven image are all of them vanity," &c.—"Thus saith the Lord thy Redeemer, I am the Lord that maketh all things, that stretcheth forth the heavens alone, that spreadeth abroad the earth by myself, that frustrateth the tokens of the liars, and maketh diviners mad."—Isa. xliv.

"Thus saith the Lord, the Holy One of Israel and his Maker, I have made the earth, and created man upon it; I, even my hands have stretched out the heavens, and all their host have I commanded.—Thus saith the Lord that created the heavens, God himself that formed the earth and made it; he hath established it; he created it not in vain; he formed it to be inhabited: I am the Lord, and there is none else.—They have no knowledge that set up the wood of their graven image, and pray unto a god that cannot save." —Isa xlv.

The foregoing conclusion respecting the creation of all things in six days, is confirmed by the narrative in the second chapter of Genesis; wherein, as in various other Scriptures, the gloss, proposed by Dr. Smith and others, on the word *made*, as though it meant *arranged*, *disposed*, or something short of *creation*, is refuted. For on the supposition that the earth was created at an earlier epoch, and that this word in the narrative of the six days refers only to the disposing, arranging, or fitting up of the chaotic materials of the pre-existing earth, we must conclude that there was no proper creation of man, or of the animals and plants, said to have been *made* in the six days.

"These are the generations [that is, the foregoing are the leading facts respecting the origin] of the heavens and of the earth, when they were *created*, in the day that the Lord God *made* the earth and the heavens [here the words *made* and *created* evidently relate to the same acts]; and *made* every plant of the field before it grew" [that is, he made the plants at the same time that he created the heavens and the earth, and made them before they grew for the reason which follows], "for the Lord God had not caused it to rain on the earth, and there was not a man to till the ground. And the Lord God *formed* man of the dust of the ground, and breathed into his nostrils the breath of life, and man became a living soul."—

Gen. ii. Elsewhere in the historical, poetical, and prophetic books, the heavens and the earth are said to have been *made*.

The geologists who profess to believe the Scriptures generally admit that there was a creation in the "six days;" a creation of man, and of the plants and animals known to subsequent history. But if the earth had been improved, during countless ages, by all the laws and agencies of nature, and was not in a state of chaos at the commencement of the six days, what does the narrative of the second and third days mean by the division of the waters, the separation of the seas from the dry land, &c.? If, on the other hand, it was in such chaotic state, how came it so? or had it during untold periods been stocked with plants and animals, without light, without rain, and without even a separation of the land from the seas, and "the gathering together of the ocean waters into one place, so that the dry land might appear."—Gen. i. 9, 10, and ii. 5.

Without pursuing further the argument from the fact that the heavens and the earth, and all things, were created *in six days*, by noticing the very numerous instances in which to renew and reiterate the remembrance of it, and the conviction of the moral and religious obligations and duties which resulted from that fact, the numbers six and seven respectively are affixed to the prescriptions respecting the tabernacle and its furniture, and to those in relation to the ritual observances, privileges, offerings, feasts, and celebrations; it is evident that the whole fabric of the Mosaic economy rests on the fact in question as its corner-stone. On that fact the claims of Jehovah as Creator, Lawgiver, and Ruler, depend. On the basis of that fact he claims the homage and obedience of men. And it is accordingly set forth most prominently at the commencement of the Scripture narrative, and reiterated as occasions arose for asserting the prerogatives and rights of which it was the basis.

The great controversy, of which hitherto this world has been the scene, which has furnished the materials of its history, and especially of that contained in the Old Testament, relates primarily and essentially only to the question, whether Jehovah the Creator, and as the Creator, or Baal the creature, was the true God, to whom the homage and obedience of all created moral agents was due. This controversy, from the apostasy to the present time, has been carried on by the great adversary, chiefly by means of idolatry, the organized, most manageable, and most effective system of antagonism and rivalship which was possible to fallen creatures. And accordingly, to rebuke and resist this system, the judgments inflicted upon rulers and people, from the Deluge to the Babylonish exile, are, in most instances, expressly declared to have been designed to cause them to know that Jehovah was the living and true God, the Creator and Moral Governor of the world.

Had the sacred writers only stated in general terms that God created the celestial bodies and the earth, without associating with that statement a detail of all the visible objects of creation, so as to exclude the idea of any other creator of any of those objects; and including in their statement man, who was to be guarded against idolatry, imposture, and error, their testimony, however correct as far as it went, would not have met the exigencies of the case.

Had the first verse of Genesis asserted the creation at an indefinitely remote, uncertain, and unknown epoch, wholly unassociated with man as a creature, and with his relations and duties as a moral agent, no such sign as the sanctification of the seventh day, to re-express and perpetuate the fact that Jehovah was the Creator, could have been instituted; nor would the bare assertion that he was the Creator, without such a significant and oft-recurring sign, founded in the details of the works of creation, and interwoven with the moral relations and obligations of man, have served to guard him against the wiles of the antagonist system.

To the same effect it may be observed, that most of

the miraculous interpositions recorded in the Old Testament are declared to have been designed to produce a conviction that Jehovah was the only living and true God, the Creator and Governor of the world, and that idols were vanity and imposture. Those interpositions were public and visible manifestations of Jehovah's supremacy and power over the objects of idolatrous homage, and over all creatures. The bare verbal assertion of such supremacy and power was insufficient. The object required acts and results which could be seen and felt, and the particulars of which could be propagated by report and recorded for perusal.

The destruction of Sodom, the miracles of Egypt, of the Red Sea, of the wilderness, the passage of the Jordan, the conquest of Jericho, and many others might be referred to. But no one is more in point than that of the arrest of the sun and moon by the Divine power through the instrumentality of Joshua. Those luminaries were the objects of the idolatrous confidence and worship of the kings and people of Canaan, who with their idol system were to be rebuked, confounded, and destroyed.

This signal exhibition of the power of the God of Israel over those celestial orbs and over the elements, occurred at a period of the war when it was most wanted to reassure and embolden the Israelites; and to dishearten and terrify the hosts of idolatry throughout the whole country. The army of Joshua had recently been repulsed and dismayed at Ai. The defection of the Gibeonites from their former allies and their league with the princes of Israel, had induced the neighboring five kings of the Amorites and their armies to march upon Gibeon with a determination to destroy it. They were aware of the total destruction of Jericho and of Ai; and when they heard that the Gibeonites had joined the invaders, "they feared greatly," and doubtless hoped by promptly destroying them to prevent further defection, and with their combined force to encounter and drive back the army of Israel. This, therefore, was to be a decisive battle. It was now to be seen whether those who trusted in idols or those who trusted in Jehovah, were to be triumphant. The great question at issue, the controversy between the God of Israel and Baal, the question which of them was superior to the other, and able to maintain his claims, was to be so tried as to foreshow and decide the issue of the whole campaign. To accomplish all this, and to strike all the other kings and armies of Canaan with terror and dismay, it was necessary not merely to exterminate the confederate Amorites, but signally and visibly to confound and triumph over their idols; as in the plagues of Egypt and the destruction of their first-born, it is said,

"Against all the gods of Egypt I will execute judgment, I am the Jehovah."

Joshua, therefore, hastened to the scene of action. The Lord said unto him, Fear them not, for I have delivered them into thy hand. And the Lord discomfited them before Israel, and showered a storm of hailstones upon them; and when the rout and the panic were at their height, at the uplifted voice of Joshua, he suspended the revolution of the earth so that the sun stood still, and the moon was stayed, until the people had avenged themselves upon their enemies—the sun stood still in the midst of heaven, and hasted not to go down about a whole day; and there was no day like that, before it, or after it—for the Lord fought for Israel!

Thus this miracle, like all other extraordinary interpositions, was wrought for adequate reasons; reasons founded in the prerogatives and moral purposes of God, and relating directly to the moral interests and duties of man. It was of a nature to be notorious and irresistibly convincing to all the idolaters on the earth. It showed that Jehovah the Creator had absolute power over the sun, moon, and earth, and all creatures, and therefore that idols were vain and impious; and it had such effect that Joshua met with but faint opposition in his subsequent triumphs; an effect which could not have been produced either upon the Israelites or upon the idolaters by a mere verbal announcement that the God of Israel was able to do such wonders.

A miracle similar in its nature and object is recorded in the history of Hezekiah, king of Judah. According to the succession of events, as narrated in Isaiah, 2 Kings and 2 Chronicles; Sennacherib king of Assyria, a zealous worshipper of Baal and his images, emboldened by the success of his grandfather and his father in subduing and carrying the ten tribes into captivity and capturing their idols; and by his own and their success in vanquishing several neighboring kings and their idol gods, invaded Judah, and sent an insolent and blasphemous message to Hezekiah and his people defying and contemning the God of Israel, as of no more power to withstand him and his idol god, than the nations and idols which he had subdued and destroyed. Jehovah, the God of Israel, vindicated his supremacy, and confounded the Assyrians and their idols, by miraculously destroying 185,000 of the invading army, and thereby freeing Jerusalem and Judea from their designs.

Owing probably to his neglect publicly to acknowledge this signal deliverance, and to celebrate the power and glory of the Deliverer, and as a censure also of his league with the idolaters of Egypt to assist him against the Assyrians, Hezekiah was visited with a mortal sickness. In answer to his earnest entreaties, his term of life was extended fifteen years; and as a sign that he should be miraculously restored, and at the same time as an exhibition of Jehovah's power over the celestial objects of idolatrous homage in Egypt and the surrounding kingdoms, he caused the sun to recede ten degrees, a space probably of about three hours, on the dial of Ahaz. The report of this prodigy was widely circulated. The princes of Babylon, the metropolis of Baal, sent ambassadors to Hezekiah "to inquire of the wonder that was done in the land." The whole fabric and hierarchy of idolatry were confounded by the annihilation of the Assyrian army, and the display of the supremacy and power of the God of Israel, over the celestial orbs.

To the same purpose, in the controversy between Elijah and the prophets of Baal, *answering by fire*, was to determine whether Jehovah or Baal was the true God. Ahab and his party worshipped the solar fire, under the idea of an intelligence residing in the sun, as the supreme ruler. To that rival intelligence and adversary they prayed, and offered human sacrifices; and to represent him when the sun was out of sight they constructed idols, molten images, in imitation of those of Egypt and surrounding nations. Elijah accordingly says to the prophets of Baal, "Call ye on the name of your Elohim; and I will call on the name of Jehovah; and the Elohim that answereth by fire, let him be Elohim."—"And they called on the name of *Baal* from morning even until noon, saying, O Baal, hear us. But there was no voice, nor any that answered."—"And Elijah said, Jehovah, Elohim of Abraham, Isaac, and of Israel, let it be known this day that thou art Elohim in Israel, and that I am thy servant, and that I have done all these things at thy word. Hear me, O Jehovah, hear me, that this people may know that thou art the Jehovah Elohim.—Then the fire of Jehovah fell, and consumed the sacrifice, &c. And when all the people saw it, they fell on their faces: and they said, The Jehovah, he is the Elohim: the Jehovah, he is the Elohim."—1 Kings xviii.

The frequent manifestation of the presence and agency of Jehovah in fire as a visible shekina, or cloud-like envelope, gave occasion probably to the antagonist and rival system. Thus, in the cherubim stationed at the gate of Eden, and doubtless in many other instances prior to the Deluge. In the more ample narrative of events after the institution of idolatry by the descendants of Noah, we have frequent notices of such Divine manifestations; as at the covenant with Abraham; in the burning bush, on Mount Sinai, in the pillar of fire, at the dedication of the tabernacle and temple; at the destruction of Nadab and Abihu; at the sacrifices of Manoah and Gideon;

and in the visions of Isaiah, Ezekiel, and Daniel. This mode of manifestation was evidently familiar to the Israelites at every period of their history; and its appropriateness as a test, when the devotees of Baal were to be confounded, is manifest. If, as required by the proposal of Elijah, Baal, the pretended fire-god, who arrogated to himself that element as his residence, the vehicle of his agency, and token of his prerogatives and power, could not, when called on, answer, and vindicate himself by fire, all men would see that he was not Elohim, but an arrogant impostor.

This high controversy which commenced with the apostacy, and is not yet terminated, was *foreseen* before the creation. The Creator himself was to be a party to it; and he took care in recording the work of creation to specify the visible objects and creatures in their several kinds, which he made; and to associate with the narrative of his acts as Creator, the exercise of his prerogatives and rights as Moral Governor, and to institute a memorial, a sign, a solemn weekly observance, with which their highest religious duties, obligations, and hopes, were indissolubly connected, to perpetuate the conviction and the most distinct and public acknowledgment, that he alone was the Creator, and that he created all things in the space of six days.

CHAPTER III.

The references to the Work of the Creation in the New, in Harmony with those of the Old Testament—Coincidence of the first verses of the Gospel of John with the first of Genesis—Incidental allusions to the Epoch of Creation—That Man and the Material Worlds were Created at the same Epoch, implied in all that Relates to the Work of Redemption, and in all the Ascriptions of Praise to the Creator for the Perfection of his Works.

THE opening of John is, both in its terms and import, the counterpart of the first verse of Genesis, "*In the beginning* was the Word; and the Word was with God; and the Word was God. The same was *in the beginning* with God. All things were made by him. —He was in the world, and the world was made by him.—And the Word was made flesh, and dwelt among us."

In these statements it was the object of the evangelist to ascribe the creation of all things to the LOGOS, the personal WORD, and thereby to attest his Divinity. He very probably had it in view to refute the Gnostic heresy, which ascribed the work of creation not to the

Deity, but to a created intelligence, or partly to a good and partly to an evil angel.

It is to be observed that he ascribes the work of creation not to the second Person in the Godhead, as such; but to that Person in the delegated, official character, in which he became incarnate, and dwelt on earth. He therefore sustained that character *in the beginning*, at the production of the first-fruits of creative energy. In that character he was with God, and "had glory with him before the world was." To assert that the second Person, as such, in distinction from his delegated character, was in the beginning, was with God, and was God, would not have subserved the writer's object, for those things could not be questioned by any who acknowledged the existence of that Person; and it would be to apply to him a name or designation applicable to his official Person only. But to say that He who appeared incarnate, and was distinguished as the Word, was in the beginning, was with God, and was God, was in every respect appropriate, as an introduction to the ascription to him of the work of creation. It was in that character that he said of himself, "before Abraham was, I am." And in the Epistle to the Colossians it is said of him, that "he is before all things, and by him all things consist."

From these considerations it is to be inferred that

the creation of all things was a part of the work delegated to the Logos, the anointed official Person; and was in order to the other works comprised in his undertaking; in the progress of which he took man's nature into union with his Person. In that view of him and his work it is written, "Thou art worthy, O Lord, to receive glory, honor, and power; for thou hast created all things, and for thy pleasure they are and were created:" and "that God created all things by Jesus Christ, to the intent that now unto principalities and powers in heavenly places might be known by (means of the redemption of) the Church, the manifold wisdom of God, according to the eternal purpose, which he purposed in Christ Jesus our Lord." And again: "For by him were all things created that are in heaven, and that are in earth, visible and invisible—all things were created by him and for him, and he is before all things."

The meaning of the phrase in the beginning, as employed by the evangelist, is evidently the same as that in Genesis i. 1. It denotes not an epoch, or anything in relation to time; but the initiatory event of a series, the first of a comprehensive plan of arrangements, agencies, and events. The statement that "in the beginning was the Word," is equivalent to saying, that the appointment of the second Person to the office of mediator, or the delegation to him in his officially subordinate Person and character of the work which he undertook, including the creation, was first in the series of measures and events which appertained to that work. He was, or existed in that official character, as the first result of his appointment. As the Anointed, the Christ, he was with God, before exercising his creative energy in the work of creation ; and in that character he created all things. Thou Lord *in the beginning* [at the commencement of thy work] hast laid the foundation of the earth, and the heavens are the work of thy hands. He was appointed heir of all things which were to be brought into existence, and as such, he made the worlds and all things to be subservient to the great moral purposes which he was to accomplish. Having created the earth, instead of leaving it through millions of ages without occupants having any relation to his moral government, he created man, and invested him with a subordinate dominion over the inferior creatures, to rule them for himself, "for whom are all things, and by whom are all things."

In this view of his person and office, and the connection of his work of creating and upholding all things with his moral and providential government, and all his works as Prophet, Priest, and King, it would be more than irreverent to represent him as having created the earth myriads of ages before he created man, whose nature, in order to the execution of the most important and glorious part of his whole uudertaking, was to be and remain forever united to his Person.

No deductions of geology, unsupported by and irreconcilable with the teachings of revelation concerning him, can justify us in disconnecting the first act in the execution of his delegated undertaking, from the series to which that, in its precedence and in all its relations, was essential.

The Scripture account makes the creation the basis and commencement of that great scheme of providence and redemption about which the entire volume of revelation is occupied. Before the foundation of the world, in that covenant transaction in which originated the office, appointment, and delegated authority, and work, of him by whom all things were created, those whom he was to redeem "were chosen in him; they were foreordained before the foundation of the world; from the beginning they were chosen to salvation;" as if all the works of creation were but means prerequisite and in order to their redemption. Accordingly he was recognized when incarnate as having sustained this delegated official character from the origin of the entire scheme of creation, providence, and grace. Hence the frequent references in his own discourses and elsewhere in the New Testament to the foundation or creation of the world as the commencement of his office and administration. He taught concerning himself and his kingdom things "which had been kept secret from the foundation of the world." "Father, I will that they also whom thou hast given me be with me where I am; that they may behold my glory which thou hast given me; for thou lovedst me before the foundation of the world." "Come ye blessed of my Father, inherit the kingdom prepared for you from the foundation of the world." "For then (if Christ offered himself periodically) must he often have suffered since the foundation of the world." "That the blood of all the prophets, which was shed from the foundation of the world, from the blood of Abel unto the blood of Zacharias—may be required of this generation." "Whose names were not written in the Book of Life from the foundation of the world." "Whose names are not written in the Book of Life of the Lamb slain from the foundation of the world." "Which God hath spoken by the mouth of all his holy prophets since the world began.—Spoken by the mouth of his holy prophets which have been since the world began." "Since the world began was it not heard that any man opened the eyes of one that was born blind." "According to the revelation of the mystery which was kept secret since the world began." "The hope of eternal life which God, that cannot lie, promised before the world began."

These quotations are somewhat multiplied, to show the current usage of Scripture in its varied and incidental references to the creation of the world as to an epoch, or stand-point, with which the commencement of the human race was coeval. No one can possibly bring himself to believe that the sacred writers in these comparisons of things present, with things done, existing, or commencing at the creation of the world, meant to refer to a creation myriads of ages prior to the creation of man; or that they did not mean to represent that the foundation, beginning, creation of the world, including man, took place at one and the same epoch—the epoch with which the first steps and pledges of the work of redemption were coincident, and to which, historically, the agency of man, the slaughter of Abel, and the mission of the earliest prophets were closely related.

In the vision, Rev. iv., which John had of the Son of God, seated on a throne encircled by a rainbow, the token of his covenant relation towards his people, and with the accompaniment of other insignia of his mediatorial office, as in the similar visions of Isaiah, Ezekiel, and Daniel, he is worshipped and praised by the elders and representatives of all his holy creatures, for having created *all things*, and having created them for his pleasure, will, or purposes, i. e., to be the scene and the instruments of his providence and grace. His worthiness to receive such homage is expressly inferred from his having created *all things*. "Thou art worthy, O Lord, to receive glory and honor and power, for thou hast created all things, and for thy pleasure they are and were created."

Assuredly the creation here referred to cannot have been the fitting up of a pre-existing earth; for the fitting up supposed by the geologists to have taken place in the "six days" was not a creation, but only a modification, by which the earth was rendered fit to be inhabited by man, after it had existed and been the abode of animals during immeasurable periods. Such modifications, even if man and certain animals were then first brought into existence, could not be called the creation *of all things*, and on that ground be made the basis of a claim to homage; for in the *all things* here, as in every parallel passage, the heavens and earth, and all their hosts, are included.

Nor can the creation referred to mean or include a creation of the earth, and certain animal and vegetable races, millions of millions of ages prior to the creation of man. For if such creation be supposed, it could have no connection with the mediatorial work, as it would have comprised no intelligent creatures, no accountable moral agents; and it is not conceivable that such agents, created myriads of ages afterwards, could have any connection with, or any relation to it. That supposed primeval earth, as the geologists teach us, was and continued to be in a state of chaos (without order, light, or life, according to Dr. Candlish), or was prior to the "six days" thrown into such a chaotic state as to exterminate all its races of plants and animals, terrestrial and marine, and render it necessary to create new races to stock anew the waters as well as the dry land. Surely it is not conceivable that such a creation, so totally disconnected with man and with the mediatorial work, should be referred to as the ground of the ascription to the Mediator of glory, honor, and power, as being for his pleasure, and subservient to the moral, providential, and redemptive work, for which he is worshipped in the scene in question, as is evident from the insignia which distinguished his appearance.

Again: the alleged primeval earth of the geologists is supposed by them to have been, if not a mere chaos, wholly without order, light, and life, yet, at best, to have been an extremely, nay, inconceivably, imperfect earth—an earth in such a state and condition as with no propriety to be called an earth, it being at first, and no one knows for how many myriads of ages, unfit for the abode of the meanest insects and reptiles, and so unfit for the abode of man, its intended prince and master, as to require a course of alterations and improvements to be carried on incessantly through immeasurable rounds of duration, before he could exist, if created or developed and brought upon the stage. After it had so far been improved by geological causes as to admit of the creation of some of the lowest organisms, the Creator interposed and brought them into existence; and when, according to the laws of their nature, which (contrary to the perfective law of the embryo earth) was a law of decay and degradation, they "died out," and took their permanent stations as organic fossils in the lowest fossilliferous stratum, the Creator interposed again, and brought forward a class of creeping things, as much more perfect than the class which had died out, as the progress of geological improvement would permit. By the repetition of this mechanical tide-waiting process, as often as the successive creations, when their places of abode became too perfect for their natures, declined and run out, the earth at last came to be stocked with animals wholly unsuited to be contemporary with man. The development had gone too far,—a retrograde movement was necessary. It was not only necessary to exterminate all the animals and vegetables, terrestrial and marine, of the latest creation, but to throw the earth itself back into a chaotic state, in order, by the operation of the "six days" spoken of by Moses, to give it just that degree of perfection which would make it suitable to the nature of man, and to stock the seas, the land, and the atmosphere, with races proper to be contemporary with him.

Wonderful scheme of operations, no doubt, considered as a geological contrivance, and as a total failure up to the epoch of the "six days." But what is to be thought of it, considered as the scheme of the Moral Governor of the Universe, who sees the end from the beginning, and acts only for reasons worthy of his infinite perfections?

Was it his object, during the untold geological cycles, to bring the incipient elementary earth, by the operation of geological causes, to such a state of perfection, that he might safely bring the creature, man, forward, under circumstances compatible with his existence? Man, the creature, on whose account alone, in distinction from all other creatures, the whole process, from the outset, was undertaken, and in comparison with whom, all other creatures were mere foils, dumb shadows, mute emblems, significant only as such, and as petrified monitors in the deep charnel-house of the earth. Man, who was to have dominion over all other creatures on the earth, "the beasts of the field, the fowls of the air, and the fish of the seas," to be brought into existence and into the scene of his imperial birthright, after innumerable creations and extinctions of distinct and entire races of his destined subjects? Man, whose terrestrial supremacy and rule, was but the emblem and reflection of the supremacy and rule over him of his Creator and Moral Governor? Man, who as head of the lower creation, was a type of the God-man as head over all things visible and invisible; to be brought into existence and into his relation of headship at the very close of a long series of distinct and widely separated creations, whose death, burial, and utter extinction, had rendered them incapable of a head!

This beggarly, earth-born scheme, is scarcely to be treated of without impatience and indignation. It dishonors every attribute of the eternal self-existent Creator; and would dishonor any human mechanician, who was competent to his undertaking. To suppose such an originally imperfect creation, is at war with all analogy in the works of the all-perfect Creator as represented in the Scriptures, and with his own emphatic attestations. It indicates nothing of wisdom or forecast; nothing of subserviency to a moral system, of the progress and consummation of which it was to be the scene. As a theory of creation, it makes man of no more significance than a reptile, distinguishing him from the inferior animals only as they are distinguished from one another by respectively requiring for their residence a more perfect habitation than their predecessors.

It is derogatory to the Creator, and a denial of his perfection, to ascribe to him the creation of anything not perfect in its kind, and not perfectly adapted to the present and prospective ends and uses for which it was designed. It is because all his works are perfect, and by their perfection brightly reflect and clearly attest his perfection and declare his glory, that he is praised and honored for them by all holy intelligences, in heaven and on earth.

Accordingly in the inspired narrative of the creation, we have the Divine attestation repeatedly expressed, that the things created then, as they came from the hand of the Creator, were good; perfect in their kind, their nature, their adaptations and relations, the product and type of the perfection which designed and gave them being. The light was *good.* The seas and the dry land were *good.* The plants and trees were *good.* The sun, moon, and stars, were *good.* The terrestrial animals, and the fish of the sea, were *good.* Man and all the animal and vegetable races, were, each according to its nature, perfect. "And God saw everything that he had made, and behold it was very good." They neither needed nor were capable of any improvement by time or by physical changes. Being the product and expression of the Creator's infinite perfection, they were rightfully, on that account, to be the occasion of ceaseless praise from all creatures. And hence the angels and hosts of heaven, the sun, moon and stars, man, and all creatures on the earth, are again and again called on "to praise the name of the Lord," for the display of his perfections in their creation; "for he commanded, and they were created; He hath also established them for ever and ever; he hath made a decree which shall not pass—Let them praise the name of the Lord; for his name alone is excellent; His glory is above the earth and heavens."—Psalm cxlviii. "O Lord, how manifold are thy works! in wisdom hast thou made them all; the earth is full of thy riches; so is this great and wide sea."—Ps. civ. "The heavens declare the glory of God [the sum of his revealed perfections], the firmament showeth the work of his hands."—Ps. xix. "Rejoice in the Lord, O ye righteous, for praise is comely for the upright. He loveth righteousness and judgment; the earth is full of the goodness of the Lord. By the word of the Lord were the heavens made, and all the host of them by the breath of his mouth. He gathereth the waters of the sea together as a heap; he layeth up the depth in store houses. Let all the earth fear the Lord; let all the inhabitants of the world stand in awe of him. For he spake and it was done, he commanded, and it stood fast."—Ps. xxxiii. "Blessed be thy glorious name, which is exalted above all blessing and praise. Thou, even thou, art Lord alone. Thou hast made heaven, the heaven of heavens with all their hosts, the earth and all things that are therein, the sea and all that is therein, and thou preservest them all; and the host of heaven worshippeth Thee."—Nehemiah ix. "Thus saith the Lord—I have made the earth and created man upon it; I, even my hands have stretched out the heavens; and all their host have I commanded. Thus saith the Lord that created the heavens; God himself that formed the earth, and made it; He hath established it; He created it not in vain; He formed it to be inhabited; I am the Lord, and there is none else. I have not spoken in secret."—Isaiah xlv.

In many of the Scriptures hitherto quoted, the creation of man is spoken of directly or by implication, in such connection with the creation of the heavens and earth as plainly to convey the idea that they were created in connection with each other at one epoch. The same idea is impressively conveyed in numerous other passages. As an example of these, at the close of the narration of the six days' operations it is said: "Thus the heavens and the earth were *finished*, and all the host of them." As much as to say, "The foregoing is an account of the commencement, progress, and completion, of the creation of the heavens, the earth, and all creatures, of course including man. For if the heavens and earth were not created within the six days, no satisfactory meaning is to be deduced from this passage considered as connected with, and as the conclusion of, the foregoing narrative. If it is supposed that the heavens as well as the earth were created at an indefinitely remote period prior to the six days, and that the above passage asserts that they were *finished* in the same sense as the geologists suppose the earth to have been finished and fitted up, then it must be inferred that the celestial orbs were at their creation imperfect like the earth, and equally needed, after an interval of incalculable duration, to be finished and fitted for the reception of their inhabitants. For it is made certain by this passage, that the *finishing* of the *heavens and earth, and all the host of them*, took place in the six days.

Again, in Gen. i. 16–19, it is said that, God *made* two great lights; the sun and moon, and the stars also; and set them in the firmament of the heaven. If this does not mean that he had made them at that epoch, and on the fourth day assigned to them their office of reflecting the light created on the first day, then the finishing of them asserted at the close of the narrative, must have included something similar to what the geologists mean by fitting up the earth, and they must, therefore, have been previously in a state of chaotic ruin, " without order, life, or light." And if they were without light, so must the earth have been, and consequently without life also; for the origin and production of light is expressly assigned to the first of the six days. Is there, then, any manifestation of the wisdom and goodness, or of any of the purposes or perfections of the Creator, in such a creation of the heavens and earth countless ages before they were finished, and rendered habitable—any such manifestation that angels and men should be specially called on to praise him for it; or such as to be with propriety alleged as the ground of his prerogatives and government over them? Had they, or have they, any real or conceivable relation to the supposed creation or its epoch? Was there any such connection between the dark and chaotic state of the earth during the supposed incalculable period, and that finishing of it, which rendered it habitable, as to extend man's responsibility back to the earlier epoch, and require him to include it in his songs and doxologies of praise?

CHAPTER IV.

Notice of some of the Physical Difficulties of the Geologic Theory—The probable quantity of matter in the Sedimentary Formations computed in cubic miles; compared with the quantity of unstratified rock existing above the sea level, and with the area of the existing oceans—The production of both Marine and Terrestrial Plants and Animals, and the Diffusion and Fossilization of them in the Sedimentary Strata, according to the Geologic theory, incredible and impossible.

Here those who believe in the inspiration of the Scriptures might be content to rest, assured that no interpretation of the facts of geology or inferences from them, in conflict with the statements of revelation, can be entitled to any consideration. But many good men, teachers of revealed religion, and others, are prepossessed with the impression that the geological theory, respecting the antiquity of the earth, is entitled to regard as a deduction or demonstration of science, and as such is in conflict with the language of Scripture. This, however, is a mistake. That which constitutes or belongs to geology as a science, has properly nothing whatever, directly or indirectly, to do with the question at issue. It has to do only with physical phenomena, their natural laws, and their physical relations and connections. To determine the Epoch of Creation is as truly out of its province as it is to create a world. It cannot demonstrate, nor even render it probable, that the earth ever was created. The theory of its remote antiquity is no part of the science, but is a discreditable appendage to it. The theory is merely an inference, a supposition, a conjecture, derived from the construction which the geologist puts upon the facts of the science, the phenomena which he observes, and the mode in which he conceives them to have been produced by the ordinary and exclusive operation of natural causes. Should he modify his inference by admitting that a supernatural cause may have been interposed to produce those facts, he would be forced to conclude that geology could determine nothing upon the subject. It is impossible for him to prove, or to exhibit any facts or phenomena from which it can be inferred that supernatural interpositions have not taken place, or that there have not been adequate reasons and occasions for them. And it is only by vaulting over the boundaries of Geological Science, into the province of revelation, moral government, and final causes, and assuming that no supernatural interpositions have occurred, that he makes his inference, and concludes that the earth must have existed long enough for natural causes to produce the phenomena which he observes.

It may be worth the while, therefore, to exhibit some of the difficulties which attend the supposition that the phenomena of geology were produced exclusively by the gradual operation of natural causes. In doing this it may perhaps appear that more miracles are required on that supposition than are indicated in the Scriptures, in connection with the physical and moral systems together.

It is not intended to advance any theory as to the mode of operation by which it pleased the Creator and Ruler of the world to produce the changes which have taken place in and beneath the surface of the earth; but only to show that the mode specified by the geologists is untenable, and to indicate that instead of physical there were moral reasons sufficient to justify the belief that they were produced by supernatural interpositions, as there undeniably have been such reasons for such interpositions in numerous instances, since the period of those changes by which the sedimentary deposits with their fossil remains were formed. This is all that the case requires. If the mode of operation is not revealed in the Scriptures, geology cannot determine it; and in relation either to our faith or practice, it is no more essential to us to know it, than it is essential to us to know the mode in which the Divine power will cause a resurrection of the dead, or to know the mode in which any physical effect is produced by a Divine Volition. It may well suffice us to know that the Scriptures set forth *moral reasons* for the great facts of sacred history, and declare that those facts were caused by the Moral Governor of the world ; as in the case of the creation itself, the deluge, the confusion of tongues, the destruction of Sodom, the exodus of the Israelites from Egypt, their deliverance, and the overthrow of the Egyptians in the passage of the Red sea, their sustentation forty years in the wilderness, &c., &c. Upon these and the like remarkable facts involving, beyond a question, supernatural interpositions, all the details of the Old Testament history absolutely depend. If they did not occur, the whole history must be a fable. If they did occur, then miracles were wrought, and wrought for the reasons assigned for their occurrence, whether the mode in which the Divine power was exercised in working them is revealed or not, and whether that mode was or was not in harmony with or in opposition to the ordinary laws of nature. And to believe in the Scriptures is to believe in those facts, and in the reasons assigned for them, and the power which caused them, as much as it is to believe in the doctrines which those facts attest concerning the Deity, the prerogatives, the moral government, the providence, the holiness, justice, and goodness, of their author. The facts occurred and were recorded purposely to attest the doctrines; they occurred under circumstances, and in such immediate connection with the reasons assigned for them, and with the doctrines they were designed to enforce, as to have the effect of the most signal attestations; and as such, the knowledge of many of them was extended over the earth, and has been perpetuated in the memories, the monuments, the languages, and the annals of the nations.

To deny, explain away, or divest these facts of their supernatural character, is to deny that the doctrines were attested by them, and to that extent, at least, to deny the doctrines themselves, and the inspiration of the record of them. Their importance and their credibility both depend wholly on their being supernatural —the immediate effect of the power of God, exerted for special and declared purposes. If they were not supernatural then they did not prove or attest any Divine truth or doctrine; and can be regarded only as stupendous fictions or childish hyperboles.

With these considerations in view, the reader will be prepared to appreciate the physical difficulties which attend the geological theory of creation. Before specifying these, however, it must be observed, that the geologists suppose the earth in its earliest and most imperfect state, to have exhibited on its surface no other substance but unstratified rock, which, unless it was originally in a state of igneous fluidity, and became solid by being cooled, is deemed to have undergone no change.

The surface of this primitive rock is supposed to have presented great inequalities of altitude and depression; the elevated portions affording materials, and the valleys space, for the sedimentary deposits in which the fossil remains of plants and animals are now discovered. The higher portions of the primitive rock, being exposed to the influence of the atmosphere and of water, are supposed to have been gradually worn away by the operation of these elements, and the abraded particles to have been washed down to the lower levels of the primitive surface, and thus gradually to have formed a stratum or layer of sediment. In process of time the first or lower stratum was covered by a second, consisting of materials geologically different from the first, as limestone differs from slate or sandstone; and that in turn was covered by a third, differing in like manner from the second; and so on through incalculable periods of duration, till the succession of layers, of which there are about thirty, attained a height of ten miles or more, from the foundation.

This process, no doubt, would require a lapse of

inconceivable rounds of time, or rather of infinite duration, on the supposition that the disintegrating agents, air and water, acted with no more force on the solid granite, than they have been observed to act during the period of secular history, or for the last 3000 years. But they are not and cannot consistently be, by the geologists, supposed ever to have acted with any more force or rapidity than at present. To suppose that they had, would be to depart from the rule of scientific induction, and introduce a higher and more powerful cause than was within their observation. The law of those agents in respect to the energy of their operation in wearing away primitive rocks, is deduced from the rate at which they are now observed to produce effects of that kind; and there is nothing in their nature to require, suggest, or admit the inference, that they were ever more powerful or effective than at present, any more than there is in the nature of gravitation anything to justify the conclusion that it once had more potency and effect than now. On the contrary, the wearing down of the rock and formation of the sedimentary deposits are supposed to have been accomplished by a process as slow as that by which the like operation is now going on. Even with respect to volcanic action, geological writers of the greatest authority allege that there is no ground to conclude that volcanoes were ever more frequent or more powerful than at present; and with respect to deluges, that while from their occurrence within the period of history we may infer that earlier ones occurred, we have no right to infer that the earlier ones were of any greater extent than the recent, of which history informs us.

Besides, if it be supposed that those causes ever operated more rapidly than at present, who can tell how much more rapidly? Was it a thousand times, or a million? or myriads of millions? Geology cannot tell; and therefore cannot decide that the effects were not produced in a brief, or comparatively brief period; in the 1600 years which preceded the deluge; in the year of the deluge; or in the next succeeding 1500 years which elapsed before the period of history commenced?

To suppose a more rapid operation of those causes ages ago, than at present, is to substitute conjecture in place of the rule of scientific induction from known facts; and if the geologist infers from the almost imperceptible action of those causes now that the effects which he considers them adapted and designed to operate, were never more rapidly produced than at present, he in so doing gratuitously assumes that no supernatural cause was ever interposed to hasten them. But such an assumption is not Science. It is mere conjecture. Geology affords no means of proving or rendering it probable that supernatural interpositions have not taken place. The utmost it can do in this relation is to show that the operation of natural causes is all but imperceptibly slow; so slow, indeed, as to render the inference that the vast masses of sedimentary matter were ever produced by them, not merely improbable and incredible, but impossible.

The question has no reference to the movement by ocean and river currents of the previously pulverized sediment with which they come in contact, but only to the operation by which the quantity of sediment is increased as well as moved; the operation by which the materials of all sediment are detached and floated away from the primitive rocks. This is all that the question does or can include. For the mere movement of soils from one locality to another does not augment the total quantity of sedimentary matter; and according to the theory there was primitive rock but no soil or other sedimentary matter when the process commenced. And this must have been the case if the theory in respect to fossil remains is true; for they are found very far down in the sedimentary strata, where according to the theory they must have been buried up by the materials which were gradually detached and washed down from the primitive rocks.

Now in order to judge whether it is in itself credible or possible, or whether without a miraculous influence upon our minds, or a hallucination equal to that which would be required to make us believe the doctrine of the Metempsychosis, we can be brought to any degree of conviction, that all the sedimentary matter of the globe has been detached from primitive rocks, by the indescribably slow operation of natural causes, disposed in the layers, and pervaded by the fossil remains now found in it; let it be observed, that the area occupied by the sedimentary formations is of vast extent. The superficial area of the globe is equal to about 148 millions of square miles; that of the dry land, or portions above the sea level, to 40 millions. Of this probably not less than four fifths, or 32 millions of square miles, are of sedimentary formation; and if that formation, as geologists of authority estimate, extends to the depth of ten miles, or more, the aggregate would be equal to 320 millions of cubic miles.

On the other hand the superficial area now occupied by primitive rock, supposed not to exceed eight millions of square miles (and more probably far less than that), cannot, it is presumed, be estimated to be on an average more than one mile in height above the general level of the adjacent sedimentary surface. For although the loftiest summits of several mountain ranges rise more than one mile and some as high as five miles, above the level of the sea, the far greatest portion of the granitic surfaces are much less than half a mile in height. Supposing the general average to be one mile in height, the result would be eight millions of cubic miles of granite above the level of the sedimentary deposits ; and the quantity of material would be equal to one-fortieth part of the quantity contained in those deposits.

Now it is to be observed that the thirty-two millions of square miles now occupied by the sedimentary masses, could not, at the commencement of their formation, nor at any period since, have furnished any of the sediment deposited there. For when the lower portion of the first layer of sediment was deposited, the same primitive rock which it now lies on must have been under it. And even if the now underlying rock yielded at first a portion of abraded particles, it would, after being covered with such particles to the depth of a few inches, be beyond the reach of the action of the agents of abrasion, and could yield no more. If then the 320 millions of cubic miles of sediment were produced by the wearing down of primitive rocks, either by the action of air and water, or by any other cause, those rocks, it is manifest, must have existed, not within, but out of and beyond the limits of the area over which the sediment was floated, and where it now remains. Those primitive rocks, if they existed anywhere, must have existed on the top of the granitic rocks which now rise above the general level of the sedimentary surfaces. They must have been piled up on the area of eight millions of square miles, assigned above to the existing granite surface; and must have exhibited an average height of forty miles; or if the most elevated summits were as much higher than the general average as the highest summits now are, there must have been granite mountains 200 miles in height, an altitude at which probably neither air nor water would ever wear them down.

It is not perceived how these conclusions can be avoided. They are not to be relieved by supposing that a process of abrasion went on for a long time over the whole area of forty millions of square miles, till a vast mass of sedimentary matter was produced from rocks within the area of thirty-two millions, before it was washed down to its destined bed. For if not washed down as fast as produced, it would stop the process of abrasion as effectually on the surface of the rock from which it was disengaged, as on the same at a lower level to which it might be floated down. And if floated down to lower levels as fast as it was disengaged, two difficulties would present themselves —1. The quantity of such rock rising above the lowest level would be exhausted or covered up long before the deposits would rise to a height of ten miles, so that there would be a vast deficiency of materials, or we must suppose such rocks to have had an elevation far greater than any of the existing primitive rocks, and to have occupied the whole or so much of the area as to preclude such extended and continuous sedimentary formations as now exist.

2. A difficulty would present itself in respect to a supply of the plants and animals terrestrial and marine, the fossilized remains of which are discovered in the lower sedimentary strata, as well as in those above. For where during the ages of such a process could plants and animals of both or indeed of either of those classes exist, so as to be supplied at the places of inhumation? Both the theory under consideration, and the facts of geology imply that the sedimentary deposits, by whatever causes effected, were in progress simultaneously, wherever they now exist, and that the presence of water was an indispensable condition of their progress. There must have been water to convey the sedimentary matter down from higher levels, and when floated down, it was evidently precipitated to its bed, in water. This would necessarily preclude the contemporaneous existence of terrestrial plants and animals; and if there was water enough to supply aquatic plants and animals, how could it at the same time supply both those of salt and those of fresh water?

The sedimentary formations are described by the geologists as consisting of not less than thirty, " well defined *beds*, *layers*, or *strata*, of *different* mineral masses, masses differing in mineral composition, lying upon each other," originally like the leaves of a book, or a pile of wafers in a horizontal position, and subsequently raised and tilted wherever their position has been altered, by a force from beneath. "They are placed one over the other, in a *sure* and *known* order of succession." Though in every locality some one or more out of the whole number of layers may be wanting, "the order of position is never violated."—*Dr. Pye Smith and others.* These well established facts are, in relation to the geological theory of formation, of great significance. The theory assumes that there were above the lower level of the first horizontal layer, primitive rocks enough to supply the entire mass of sedimentary matter, and of course if the first layer was universally horizontal in its position, that entire mass must have existed elsewhere than over the area of the first sedimentary deposit. That first layer being everywhere the same, and diverse in mineral composition from the layer above it, must be supposed to have been in progress of formation universally at the same time. For if it was not, then, since the surface of the rock from which all the sedimentary matter was to be derived, was, wherever it existed, universally exposed to the agents of disintegration, the operation of those agents must, in relation to some localities, have been miraculously suspended, while it went on wherever the first layer was in progress. For these physical agents or causes could not suspend themselves, nor choose where to operate. It is their nature, their inherent and invariable law, to operate whenever and wherever they come in contact with the physical subject upon which it is their nature to have any influence. And if those primitive rocks existed, their entire surface must have been exposed to those agents, for by the theory no portion of the globe originally exhibited any other solid surface but primitive rock, and the operation of those agents on that surface must have been everywhere the same; it could not be wholly or partially suspended without a miracle.

Now if all the solid part of the globe which is not occupied by the sedimentary deposits was granite, and was worn down to supply the materials of those deposits; if the wearing down and deposition were universally in progress at the same time, if the materials detached from the rock were floated to the scene of their final destination, and there suspended in water, diffused over the whole area, and quickly precipitated to the bottom, so as to form in course of time the first layer, and subsequently the other layers in their due order and succession, then, beyond all question, there was during that process no place on the earth for the production of plants and animals to be buried up. To suppose that there was, is to assume that the physical causes of disintegration were not universally in operation, but were suspended, which required a miracle. If they were not suspended, if they continued to work their effects upon the rock, what became of the detritus? Was the washing down suspended also, by another miracle? If so, and the materials, after being disengaged by air and water, or by air alone, were left on the rock and there accumulated till a soil was formed for the growth and support of plants and animals to be subsequently transported to another scene and buried up, that course of things would defeat itself; for a slight accumulation of sedimentary matter on the elevated rock, as well as on that beneath the sedimentary beds, would prevent the abrading agents from coming in contact with the rock to be worn down, and wholly stop the supply of materials for covering up the plants and animals, or for going on with the sedimentary formation without them.

There is no alternative to this course, but that of allowing more time and introducing more miracles. For if the washing down of sedimentary matter was suspended till a soil was formed for plants and animals, a miracle must occur to bring them into existence at the proper time; when they were to be buried up, a miracle or something like it must occur to renew the floating down of the soil, lay the primitive rock bare again, and transport the plants and animals to the place of burial. And when this was accomplished, the washing down must be again suspended, and a new soil being formed, a new creation of plants and animals must take place. In this way only can the theory be sustained, and accordingly the geologists tell us of new creations and centres of creation as often as the exigencies of their theory require them.

Nor can this theory be relieved of its impossible conditions or its dependence on miracles by the supposition that the sedimentary masses were formed on the bed of the seas, and subsequently elevated above their surface. It would be equally true upon that as upon the former suppositions, that the primitive rock which was to furnish the whole quantity of sedimentary matter, must have existed elsewhere than within the area occupied by it after the process of deposition in strata or layers; and wherever those rocks existed above the sea level, the process of wearing them down and floating the detached sediment to the sea, would equally preclude the growth of plants and animals to be inhumed.

Moreover, if the seas were deep enough to admit of their receiving sediment to the height of ten miles, the intrusion of such a mass would necessarily displace an equal bulk of water, and thereby raise the general surface, or overflow all but the most elevated portions of the earth's surface not previously submerged. But waiving all this, is it not inconceivable and impossible without a miracle, that the sediment detached from primitive rocks and washed down by river currents, should by the force of those currents or by any other means, be diffused and precipitated equally over the areas covered by the seas? Are there currents in the seas extending in all directions from the mouths of rivers? Currents of such extent and force, and in such variety as to transport materials coarse and fine, ponderous and light, thousands of miles, and distribute in different localities such only as were homogeneous, and to transport and diffuse also the plants and animals whose fossilized remains are now discovered? Surely the miracles of Scripture are nothing, compared to those which are necessary to this hypothesis. For supposing that the slow operation of natural causes might, during the lapse of an infinite succession of ages, wear down a quantity of primitive rocks equal in bulk to the sedimentary formations, it is demonstrable that there was not on the globe room for that quantity of rocks to exist, out of the space occupied by those formations, and the space occupied by the waters of the ocean; and it is equally plain that if such a process was carried on according to the uniform law of those causes, and by means of water as the principal of them, the growth of plants and animals must have been precluded till those formations were completed, so that their remains could not possibly be distributed and fossilized in the respective strata.

Whether the theory of the geologists, as specified above, is in all its particulars held and agreed to by all of them, or not, is in no degree important. For while they may differ among themselves in regard to the nebular hypothesis, which by some is deemed to have been exploded by the telescopes of Lord Rosse, but which, being mere conjecture, and never having had a particle of evidence, science, or scientific induction to support it, needed no explosion; and while they may differ as to the equally gratuitous hypothesis of the earth having been originally in a melted state, a state of "igneous fluidity:" or as to the question whether or not the fossil remains in the lowest fossiliferous stratum are those only of the most imperfect specimens of organic developments, and those of the next and of the superior strata in their order, of more perfect specimens; or whether they agree or differ as to any other details of their unscriptural and incredible system; they one and all agree in those assumptions, inferences, and dogmas, upon which their system, as such, must stand or fall. They one and all agree in supposing that the sedimentary masses were formed by the ordinary gradual operation of physical causes; that the sediment was provided by the wearing down of unstratified rock; that there have been successive creations of animal and vegetable races; that the fossil remains of plants and animals were imbedded in the sediment as it gradually washed down; that this gradual, and all but imperceptibly slow process, must have continued through infinite, or all but infinite periods of duration; and therefore that the earth must have existed, indefinitely earlier than the "six days" of the Mosaic narrative. This last particular, which is the top stone of their theory, is their inference from the preceding assumptions.

The theory is mere matter of conjecture. The notion that the solid surface of the globe was at first all rock, is mere conjecture. Geology can furnish no evidence whatever that any portion of the surface was at first rock of any kind. It cannot show that all the primitive rock which now appears, or ever has appeared, has not been raised up from beneath the general level, since the operation of geological changes and of sedimentary formations commenced. On the contrary, the notorious facts that sedimentary rocks and fossil remains are found in different countries on the summits of the most elevated mountains, where perpetual congelation has preserved them from abrasion; and that the granite surface of Sweden is reported to be gradually rising at the present time, might rather justify the conclusion that all the primitive rocks have in like manner been raised, and within a period not more remote. If the loftiest masses have been so raised, who can say that those of inferior height have not? It may give the reins to speculation, and may conjecture, that the earth was formed by the operation of mechanical and chemical forces, of what is called nebular matter; but can offer no semblance of evidence that such was its origin; that it was at first in a state of igneous fluidity, and that the crust when it cooled was granite; but it can offer nothing of the nature of proof to that effect. On the contrary, the facts that melted matter thrown up from below the crust by volcanic action is not granite when it cools, and that lava cannot be made of granite without other ingredients, might at least suggest the probability that the granite crust was never in a melted state.

It may conjecture that the plants and animals which are fossilized were provided somewhere, but cannot tell where; that they were transported somehow to their destined places, but cannot tell how; that being transported they were by some means kept in a perfect state without injury to their most fragile parts and delicate tissues, long enough for the accumulation of sedimentary matter by the action of natural causes to bury and fossilize them, but cannot show by what means.

CHAPTER V.

Notices of some portions of the Chapter "On the bearing of Final Causes on Geologic History," in the "Foot-prints of the Creator," by Hugh Miller—His inference of successive creations from the relative proportion of Brain to the Spinal Cord in different races of Animals—His version of the Fourth Commandment.

The sagacious author of the work entitled "Foot-prints of the Creator," has constructed an argument favorable to the hypothesis that man was brought forward upon the scene of terrestrial things long after the creation and extinction of the inferior races whose remains are entombed in the nether rocks; founded upon the notion that "the large reasoning brain" by which he is distinguished, "would have been wholly out of place in the earlier ages;" namely, the ages during which those inferior races had their career, and were fossilized. For he supposes that during those ages this planet was but partially consolidated, and was the scene of convulsions and earthquakes which would have frightened man and dethroned his reason, but which might have been endured by "animals of a limited range of instinct." "Fishes and reptiles," he observes, "were the proper inhabitants of our planet during the ages of the earth-tempests; and when under the operation of the chemical laws these had become less frequent and terrible, the higher mammals were introduced. That prolonged ages of these tempests did exist, and that they gradually settled down, until the state of things became at length comparatively fixed and stable, few geologists will be disposed to deny." He then cites the upheaved and distorted condition of various rocks as evidence that they were forced into that condition by movements of terrific violence, at periods when such violence was common; and adds; "The reasoning brain would have been wholly at fault in a scene of things in which it could neither foresee the exterminating calamity while yet distant, nor control it when it had come; and so the reasoning brain was not produced until the scene had undergone a slow but thorough process of change, during which, at each progressive stage, it had furnished a platform for higher and still higher life. When the coniferæ could flourish on the land, and fishes in the seas, fishes and cone-bearing plants were created; when the earth became a fit habitat for reptiles and birds, reptiles and birds were produced; with the dawn of a more stable and mature state of things, the sagacious quadruped was ushered in; and, last of all, when man's house was fully prepared for him—when the data on which it is his nature to reason and calculate, had become fixed and certain,—the reasoning, calculating brain, was moulded by the creative finger, and man became a living soul. Such seems to be the true reading of the wondrous inscription chiselled deep in the rocks. It furnishes us with no clue by which to unravel the unapproachable mysteries of creation; these mysteries belong to the wondrous Creator and to Him only. There is no geological fact nor revealed doctrine with which this special scheme of development does not agree."—P. 303.

Now if there is any legible inscription chiselled in the rocks, and if the author has translated it correctly, it reveals to us that there were successive creations of plants and animals at widely distant intervals. During the ages of this process, "Nature lay dead in a waste theatre of rock, vapor, and sea, in which the insensate laws, chemical, mechanical, and elastic, carried on their blind, unintelligent processes."—P. 330. "The *creative fiat* went forth," and the dynasty of the fish was introduced. Many ages subsequently, "*through an act of creation*, the dynasty of the reptile began;" and so of the rest.

Only assume that the author's reading of the inscription is the true one, and that there are unapproachable mysteries of creation, to which this earliest and most recondite revelation affords no clue, and to which, of course, the Mosaic narrative cannot be deemed to have any reference, and, we may forsooth, confess our ignorance of the whole matter, and quietly take up with any geological hypothesis which may be proposed. If there is anything of the slightest importance to be known by us about the creation which is not recorded in the Holy Scriptures; if it concerns us to know the mode in which physical effects are produced by the Divine will; if the inspired record of the great moral reasons and purposes for which the work of creation was accomplished, will not suffice us; if the Scripture account of the creation relates only to the last of a long succession of creations; if no account of these earlier creations is vouchsafed to us, except that which is inscribed in the rocks, and the meaning of that can only be guessed at and assumed as one most conformable to a preconceived theory concerning the rocks themselves; then it would be modest in us to be content with our total ignorance of the matter, and confine ourselves within the legitimate and well-known limits of scientific observation and induction.

It would be very easy for a geologist of half Mr. Miller's abilities, half his capacity of observation, his powers of analysis, and his exuberance of invention, and resource, to demolish his chapter on Final Causes without taking more than half as much liberty of assumption and conjecture as he takes. He betrays indubitable tokens of being spell-bound, to the extent of infatuation, by the foregone conclusion of his theory concerning the high antiquity of the earth and the succession of animal and vegetable creations. In that conclusion, as a geological inference, he is immovably fixed; and if it palpably conflicts with the text of Scripture, and the geological inscription on the rocks is so far illegible or equivocal as to require a comment, he is enough infatuated to endeavor to support it by such hypotheses and conjectures as his prolific imagination can supply. One must conceive him to have pored so intently over geological phenomena as to have become insensible to things of another sort beyond them. Like some men of trade, of whom it is said that the penny which they see is in such close contact with their visual organ, as to eclipse and render them insensible to the guinea beyond. It is quite possible, no doubt, for a good man to allow his mind to be so engrossed by physical studies, so imbued with the feelings, associations, fellowships, and theories, connected with them, as to keep all other things out of it, or allow them only a subordinate, occasional, and unimportant share of his attention. And by degrees he may come to think that the physical things which fall under his observation are in themselves of the first importance, and that the puzzling questions which they suggest require to be resolved in order to clear up the mysteries of the universe; that they present themselves at the very outset of inquiry, and must be accounted for by some theory, hypothesis, or conjecture, in order to any understanding of the nature of things. And if his studies are geological, and conduct him down into the bowels of the earth, the foundations, foot prints, and first beginnings of the operations of nature, he may easily persuade himself that he is there to discover not merely the first rudiments of things, but a record and revelation of the causes and operations by which they came to be what they are, and the reasons and orderly succession of their changes. To have found a record which he could not decipher, into some hypothesis which geology at least could not absolutely disprove, would perplex and humble him, and disrobe his science of nearly all which makes it the admiration of one portion of the world, and the stumbling-block and scandal of another.

Had the same good man, however, commenced his course of studies concerning the works of the Creator, in another school and in another class; had he commenced not with the study of insensate laws and blind unintelligent processes; but with things which are as intelligible and as certain as are the axioms of geometry, things taught by the Creator himself, in language of his own inditing, of which the laws are as fixed and as invariable as those of any science; had he begun by ascertaining what is thus taught concerning the creation, its epoch, its connections and relations with the moral purposes, agencies, manifestations, and results, of the great scheme of Providence and redemption; had he in tracing the progress of this scheme noted the occurrence of supernatural interpositions, and the reasons of them and their subserviency to moral ends; and duly considered the apostasy of man, the terrestrial head of his and the inferior races, the visitation of moral and physical judgments consequent thereon, the curse upon the earth itself on his account, not by the gradual operation of natural laws tending to improve it, but by the direct judicial agency of Omnipotence, changing it from its perfect paradisiacal condition in which it was suited to be the perpetual abode of man in his perfect, happy, unfallen state, to a condition corresponding to his fallen, degraded, miserable condition of guilt, condemnation, disease, and death, and without supernatural interposition, of utter and eternal despair; had he traced this line of things down to the removal of the curse, the restitution of all things, the resurrection of the dead and the coincident renovation of the earth and re-instatement of it in its original condition; had he taken this course of inquiry, and fully satisfied and convinced himself of what the inspired volume reveals concerning it before he attempted to construe the pretended inscrip tion and fancied revelation of the rocks, he would have had something to go by upon which he could place reliance, something to admonish him of the insignificance of physical in comparison with moral and spiritual things, something to maintain upon his mind a constant impression of the majesty and glory of the Creator, of his perfections as displayed in all his works, of the transcendent moral purposes and ends of his entire administration; something to restrain him from lawless theorizing and conjectural hypothesis.

In the author's chapter above referred to, on " The Bearing of Final Causes on Geologic History," many shrewd and fine things are said; but so far as it attempts to explain anything which the Scriptures have not explained, or advances explanations different from those vouchsafed in Scripture, it assumes what cannot be proved, exalts the rocks and their relics far above their proper place in the great system of things, disparages the inspired record, the existence of which is far more matter of wonder than all the physical phenomena of earth, and is in short mere hypothesis and conjecture. Let it be judged of by a further notice of that part of the chapter from which extracts are quoted above, and a notice of another portion which relates to the fourth commandment.

In the quoted extracts and their connections the author first assumes, in support of the hypothesis, that the earth was originally in a state incompatible with the existence of any animal or vegetable life, and that at successive stages of improvement successive creations took place, and corresponding extirpations of those which preceded to make room for those which followed; that as the brain in fishes bears an average proportion to the spinal cord of not more than two to one, while the brain in reptiles bears an average proportion of two and a half to one, in birds of three to one, and in mammals of four to one, therefore being best adapted by having the smallest modicum of brain, to exist in the most imperfect state of the earth compatible with animal life, fish were created first; and having run their course, died out and been buried, and petrified in the sedimentary rocks which now contain their relics, gave place at the next stage of improvement to their more intelligent or more sensitive, or at least larger-brained successors, the reptiles; and these in like manner, after the necessary lapse of ages, gave place to birds, and they in turn to beasts, and they to man, whose brain bears an average proportion to the spinal cord of twenty-three to one. If this theory be true, there ought not to be any fishes or reptiles now in the improved earth. Taking this graduated scale of proportionate quantity of brain as the rule of creative interposition, corresponding to the degree of improvement in the condition of the earth, the author is met by the Lamarckian theory, that "the lower brains were developed into the higher;" which he rebukes by observing that "all the facts of geological science are hostile to it," and alleging that fishes though created first, and being lowest in the proportion of brain, are in fact as a class of animals *superior to reptiles*, so that a development of the fish into the reptile would be a reverse process, a development from the more to the less perfect, which could never result in quadrupeds or man. But what now has become of the assumed rule of creative action, by which the most stupid races were to be created and have their great geologic period, before the less stupid, so as to coincide with the assumed stages of improvement in the condition of the earth? Either it was no rule, or it was violated. And if the reason why one race had less brain than another, was that they might exist and endure the tempests of their geologic cycle, then there was a mistake in the allocation of the fish. Had Baal been the Creator, and waited a million or two of ages for the insensate laws of matter to improve the earth up to the exact point where an immediate creation of newts and serpents was called for, some plausible excuse for his blunder might be devised. It might be urged as in another case of his delinquency, "he is a god," though absent; "either he is talking, or he is pursuing, or he is on a journey, or peradventure he sleepeth and must be awaked."

But the blunder is far worse for the geologic theory than it proved to be for the nimble creatures upon whom the first experiment of life was tried, for they survived the storm which raged beneath and over them, went the round of their circle, died and were entombed; and thus furnished us with good and sufficient evidence that the theory is false; that the capacity of enduring the shock of tempests does not depend upon the relative quantity of brain to the spinal cord. For if it is conceded, and affirmed, as it is by our author, as a fact so notorious and indisputable as to overthrow the Lamarckian theory of development, that fishes with the lowest proportion of brain are superior to reptiles with one fourth or twenty-five per cent. more of brain; and though so decidedly superior in all that the brain can be the means of, are yet better adapted to battle with the crude condition of things and the terrific storms of the first epoch of life, and therefore were created first, then the rule of creative action was not deduced from the proportion of any given quantity of brain to any foreseen or unavoidable severity of tempests. And if the most stupid creatures could, by reason of their stupidity, exist at the most imperfect stage of improvement of the planet, and endure the tempests of that stage better than any more sensitive class of creatures, then there was no occasion to wait for the lapse of ages of further improvement of the planet, before creating the reptiles. They might have been created at the same time with the fish as well as not, and lived contemporaneously as they do now. Indeed they would have had the best of it. For on the coming on of a storm from overhead, they could retreat to the water; and in case of a tempest from beneath they could take to the solid earth, which the fishes could not do.

Moreover, if the reptiles with twenty-five per cent. more of brain than the fish, could live under the same circumstances as the latter, then who knows but that the bird with only twenty per cent. more brain than the reptile, and the mamifer with only one third more brain than the bird, might live very well, as they now do, under the same circumstances?

It should be considered that it is only the most perfect of these several classes that had so large a proportion of brain beyond the maximum of their inferiors respectively. The least perfect probably had very little more than the best of the next inferior class; so that a goose or a turkey buzzard would have little if any more brain than a sprightly pike or a cuttle-fish, and less than a bird-catching snake or a boa-constrictor; and the woodchuck and the donkey might have less than the highest specimens of reptiles and birds.

On what account it is, since it is not in quantity of brain, that the author considers the fishes superior to the reptiles of those most ancient creations, he does not state. The fact, however, if it be one, is important, since it strikes a physical death-blow to the development hypothesis. And who knows but that the reptiles, having obtained the birthright of the fishes, as Jacob obtained that of Esau, held the privilege ever afterwards? A degree of probability to that effect might be inferred from the historical narrative of the only creation of reptiles of which we have any inspired account. For in that account the reptile, whatever may have been true as to the dimensions of his brain, appears in some other particulars to have been superior not only to the fishes but also to the mammiferous quadrupeds—"the serpent was more *subtle* than any beast of the field."

If the reader is not fully satisfied that this brain theory is untenable, considered as having any possible relation to the hypothesis of successive creations and corresponding improvements of the earth by the swathing and wet-nursing of blind, unintelligent, insensate laws of dead matter, let it be considered in another aspect.

The theory assumes that the earth, from a state originally of utter imperfection, went on improving in its condition and fitness to be the platform of organized existence through a countless succession of ages, while the animal races brought on to it successively as it became fit to be their habitation, became from the dawn of their existence subject *to a process of decline and degradation*, under which they grew more and more imperfect till they could no longer live, and so one after another of them "died out." It seems at first a little singular that the dead earth should go on improving, and by improving get fit for living creatures, and that the living creatures being produced as soon as it was fit for them, should be subject to a reverse, retrograde law; and probably the hypothesis would have contained no such provision had it not been necessary to clear the platform for new creations. There would have been no necessity for new creations, had the first races continued without degenerating and running out. But new creations are absolutely indispensable to the geologic hypothesis of antiquity. The very high antiquity of the earth in comparison with the Scripture epoch, being the essential point, it is necessary that the hypothesis should treat the matter as though the creatures were made for the earth and the geological argument, and not the earth for the creatures.

But this instructive portion of the hypothesis has a bearing on the brain theory. This latter theory teaches that a reptile is perfect as one of his class, or as perfect as his nature permits, when his brain bears to his spinal cord the proportion of two and a half to one; the bird of three to one; the beast of four to one; and man of twenty-three to one. With that proportion they exhibit the perfection of their natures; but without it, or with any considerable excess or defect, there would be a redundancy or want of those faculties or capacities depending on the brain, which distinguish respectively the several races and the individuals of each race.

Now is it the brain and its relative proportion of size which constitutes this distinguishing characteristic, or is it something distinct from the brain, of which that organ may be an instrument, but on which, and especially on its relative dimensions, it has no dependence whatever? Consider this question with reference to reasoning man, on the supposition that the average proportion of his brain to his spinal cord is as twenty-three to one. Does his power of reasoning depend in any degree upon that proportion, or any proportion approximating to that? Is it not notorious that considerable portions of that material substance may be withdrawn by the instruments of surgery, and that the whole of it, except a shrivelled figment, may be dissipated by disease without impairing the subject's power of reasoning? Is it not well known that the like operations may take place in the lower animals without impairing any of their previous faculties? And if this may happen to some individuals of the several races, it might happen to many, and to all, without affecting in any degree their capacity to endure the alleged earth tempests. And so far as the dimensions of his brain were concerned, man might as well have been created at the same epoch with the beasts and birds. The size of his brain did not decide his fitness as a reasoner, for a particular stage of improvement in the condition of the earth. That he had, in a higher degree than the inferior races, that something distinct from the brain, which employs the brain as one of its instruments, and that that something had proportionably more to do in his case than in the other cases, so as to require an instrument relatively larger, may all be very true. But he might have been fully as much frightened, and his reason fully as much confounded by a sudden, unforeseen, and resistless outburst of storm and tempest, with half his quantity of brain as with the whole of it. In other words, a necessity of his having a given quantity of brain in order to his being a reasoner, and the incompatibility of his having that amount of brain and reasoning, with a tempest-tossed state of the earth, could not have been a reason for postponing his creation till the tempests were over. Probably the relation of the brain in the lower races and in man, to that something of which the brain is an instrument, is one of the unapproachable mysteries of creation which the geological hypothesis does not unravel. And it is pitiful and abominable for a geologist, an author, and a magnate in the science of geology, to confound that incomprehensible relation with the brain itself, and make it the basis or an essential element of an hypothesis of successive creations.

The simple truth in the case is, that there were no successive creations, and of course there were no reasons for them, nor any evidences of them. They exist only in fanciful conjectures, inferences, and hypotheses; and other geologists, as well as this author, in speculating about them, inconsistently cross their own track and confute themselves. They are all occasionally like Lamarck, who "had a trick of dreaming when wide awake, and calling his dreams philosophy."—*Footprints.*

According to the geological theory the higher orders of animals chronologically succeeded the lower; and first, when the earth was sufficiently improved to permit their existence, fishes were created, and during their "dynasty" no superior class of creatures was brought upon the stage. In course of time they degenerated and died out; their remains were imbedded in the rocks, and their dynasty was thus closed and ended. Next, at a more improved period of the planet, "the dynasty of the reptiles" had its beginning, progress, and termination in like manner. Then followed the creation, reign, and extinction of the birds, and after them the dynasty of the beasts. Now if we follow these successive dynasties down to their graves, we ought to find conclusive evidence that they were buried as soon as they died, or at least before their successors were created and put in possession of their former dwelling-place. And so beyond a question they must have been, if they died, and died out, and if their inhumation was effected in the way described by the geologists. For their remains, uninhumed, could not without a miracle be preserved through a long tract of ages to be then entombed side by side with the remains of dynasties succeeding them, and in sedimentary beds formed long after their career of life and rule had ceased. None of them, not one of them, if the theory is true, ought to be found, or is or could be found in any higher or other sedimentary stratum, than that which was formed for their sepulchre, during the continuance of their life and reign. For the interval between the supposed successive creations was, by the theory, immensely long, millions of ages perhaps, or more, during which the sedimentary deposits went on to improve the earth up to the fit point of the coming dynasty; and if it went on, and the first creation died off, its relics must have been buried up before the relics of the second creation were deposited. But what do the geologists tell us? Why, they honestly announce the fact, inconsistent as it is with their theory, that the relics of these successive "dynasties," instead of having been buried as they should have been to sustain the theory, in their respective and proper places of sepulture, are found more or less diffused and mixed with each other in the formations of the supposed successive periods.

In the Silurian group of sedimentary rocks, which is next to the lowest, marine shells, crustacea, and various *fishes* are found. In the next group, the carboniferous, are *fishes*, *reptiles*, insects, and fresh-water shells. In the next, the red sandstone, are *fishes*, *reptiles*, *birds*, crustacea, &c. In the next group, the oolitic, are *fishes*, *reptiles*, *birds*, *quadrupeds* (mammalia), cetacea, crustacea, insects. Then in the cretaceous and tertiary groups, are *fishes*, *reptiles*, *birds*, *mammalia*, crustacea shells, insects. So that the several classes, the fancied "dynasties" of fishes, reptiles, birds, and beasts, instead of being respectively created, living, dying, and being buried each in a period chronologically and widely separated from the others, were, as their relics unequivocally testify, created at one and the same epoch, and lived, and died, and were buried together in one and the same comprehensive period. Fishes, reptiles, and birds, are found in rocks formed long after they, by the theory, ceased to exist, and were consigned to their last home ; and mammalia are found in rocks formed before they were created, as well as after they became extinct.

The poetry of brain-disturbing storms and tempests, might therefore have been spared. There was no need to marshal all the blind insensate forces of nature, chemical, mechanical, atmospheric, aquatic, plutonic, galvanic, electric, to terrify the dynasties of smaller or larger brains, as the eruption of hordes of starving Cossacks terrifies the slumbering hamlets which they come to sack.

The same conclusion results from another consideration ; namely, that the supposed violent action of those physical forces in producing earthquakes and volcanic tempests, and thereby, according to the theory, elevating and distorting the stratified masses, could not have taken place till after the several groups of sedimentary rocks with their fossil relics were deposited. This is demonstrated beyond a question, by the fact that those groups, which all agree were formed in a horizontal position by the precipitation of sediment in water, are in their due order and connection, tilted up together to different degrees of inclination, in different localities, and in many instances to a vertical position, which shows that the disturbing forces from beneath must have been dormant till the formations were complete. For if the lowest fossiliferous stratum had been upheaved during the fish dynasty, or that and the next during the reptile, the superior ones could not have been deposited on them, or afterwards tilted to a conformable position. The whole process of sedimentary formation must undoubtedly have been completed, before any tilting up of the lowest and the highest groups together could take place, consistently with their present actual position. And therefore it cannot possibly be true that the fishes were created ages before the reptiles, the reptiles ages before the birds, and the birds ages before the beasts; and of course their respective quantities of brain could not have been intended to fit them for any foreseen intensity of earth tempests. On the contrary they must have had a calm and quiet time during their lives, deaths, and burials.

It is remarkable how the minds of men, and even of good men, when so engrossed and enamored with theories and speculations in physical science, as to fancy that there is in its phenomena and its laws a

competency to guide them, and an intelligibleness and authority, or at least an intelligibleness, superior to the written revelation, easily adopt and become reconciled to constructions of the inspired record, palpably inconsistent with its import as read in conformity with the known, legitimate, and established laws of language. In such cases they practically exalt what they deem the testimony of nature, above the testimony of the omniscient Creator; and under the scarf and hood of science as priestly vestments, seem to idolize nature, and in derogation of the second article of the Decalogue, to bow down to things in the earth and in the waters under the earth. They become imbued with a superstitious reverence of physical nature and science, and the claims and teachings of inspiration are obscured to their view. The customary exclusion from their inquiries, recognitions, and theories, of all that is supernatural, tends to generate a prejudice and aversion against the miracles of Scripture. And hence it happens, with geologists for example, and perhaps without exception, that when, out of deference to their conclusions, they reject or explain away the plain import of the Mosaic narrative of creation, in respect to its epoch, its comprehensiveness, or other particulars, they find it easy to reject the narrative of the deluge, in respect to its universality, and its effects as a visitation of judgment on the earth; and in like manner to reject or lightly esteem the record of other supernatural interpositions. And they appear to do this under the impression that they are all the more consistent believers of the Bible, as being the truest interpreters of its meaning.

Without observing these things with any special reference to the gifted author of the "Foot-prints of the Creator," his exegesis of the fourth commandment may yet be noticed as an illustration of what is meant. Being firmly fixed in the geologic conclusions, that in the course from stage to stage, of the elevatory process of physical improvement of the earth, there had been successive creations, he readily brings himself to think, that the "six days" in which the Lord made the heavens and the earth, the sea and all that in them is," represent the immense periods which intervened between those stages of improvement; that the seventh day on which the Creator rested, represents the ensuing period, including the present and all future time; and that the reason why man was required to keep every seventh natural day of twenty-four hours, was simply a reason of *proportion*. Accordingly he proposes the following version, or substitution, in which he "sees no absurdity;" "Six *periods* shalt thou labor and do all thy work; but on the seventh *period* shalt thou do no labor, thou nor thy son, &c.; for in six *periods* the Lord made heaven and earth, the sea and all that in them is, and rested the seventh *period;* therefore the Lord blessed the seventh *period*, and hallowed it." Because the Creator did all his work in six periods of immense duration, and rested throughout the whole remaining period of time, present and future; therefore, man was to labor, and do all his work in six natural days, and wholly cease from labor on the seventh. But supposing the natural days to bear the right *proportion* to the *periods*, or maintain the proportion of six days and periods, to seven, concinnity would seem to demand in carrying out the parallel, that man should never do any more work after the first six days of his life, and that having rested the seventh natural day, we should hear no more of him. But the author's hypothesis and his ingenuity help him over this small difficulty. Being sure that the six days of creation were six periods, and consequently that the ensuing day of rest, inasmuch as a day of twenty-four hours would be out of all proportion to the six periods of duration, was a period, although future, of duration corresponding to those which preceded it, he thinks that man's day of rest may have been intended to include the whole of his natural life; and in that view of the case we must of course conclude that it was to be a day of seven periods of incessant labor. But hear him; for though generally a lucid writer, he is not altogether so as a commentator. "God rested on the *Sabbath*, and sanctified it; and therefore man ought also to rest on the *Sabbath*, and keep it holy. But God's *Sabbath* of *rest* may still exist; *the work of Redemption may be the work* [rest!] *of his Sabbath day*. That elevatory process through successive acts of creation which engaged him during myriads of ages, was of an ordinary week day character; but when the term of his moral government began, the elevatory process proper to it assumed the Divine character of the Sabbath. This special view appears to lend peculiar emphasis to the reason embodied in the commandment. The collation of the passage with the geologic record seems, as if by a species of re-translation, to make it enunciate as its injunction, 'keep this day, not merely as a day of memorial related to a past fact, but also as a day of co-operation with God in the *work* of elevation in relation both to a *present* fact, and a future purpose.' God keeps his Sabbath, it says, in order that he may save; keep yours also, that you may be saved! It serves, besides, to throw light on the prominence of the Sabbatical command, in a digest of law of which *no part or tittle* can pass away until the fulfilment of all things. During the present *dynasty* of probation and trial, that special *work* [rest!] of both God and man, on which the character of the future *dynasty* depends, is the Sabbath day *work* [rest?] of saving and being saved." The author must have forgotten, for a moment, while writing this exposition, that the Sabbath day was sanctified for man, immediately after the six days' work of creation was finished, when man was perfect, and needed no elevatory process, and when, not having apostatized, he needed no salvation. And though he may have been physically awake, he must have been mentally asleep, and dreaming, when he collated the fourth commandment with the geologic record, so as to make it, "by a species of re-translation," enunciate a meaning wholly diverse and contrary to its meaning in the inspired record of Moses, as read and construed in conformity with the uniform laws of language. The beasts, whose predecessors figure so largely in "the geologic record," are in this geological re-translation of Moses, most unwarrantably overlooked; and at least virtually denied any Sabbath whatever, since being saved is not predicable of them. The command says, "In the seventh day thou shalt not do any *work*, thou nor thy—cattle."

A more preposterous, not to say reckless and irreverent jumble of words and ideas, than this exposition contains, is surely nowhere to be found, unless it be in the fancied inscription in the nether rocks. It is so surcharged with absurdity, as neither to appear absurd to its author, who saw only through the opake glass of fossil relics, nor to require any lengthened refutation. With such liberty of imposing any meaning on the sacred text which any theory or hypothesis may require, the Bible may be made to support all the errors and false theories which have ever been put forth, and one as well as another. It were far better, far more modest, far less hurtful, not to attempt to reconcile the Scriptures with a theory which requires such palpable and outrageous perversion of their plainest passages, their precepts and moral laws which involve the moral and religious obligations, and the eternal interests of man. If such passages, a punctilious practical obedience to which was required on pain of death, may be explained to mean anything or nothing, to suit a physical theory, then the Bible is, as to its meaning, the most uncertain of all books, or, rather it has no meaning, and is wholly unworthy of confidence. And in regard to Moses and the Moral Law, we are left to infer that if he had known what our geologists know of the inscription and revelation in the rocks of bygone ages, he would have revised and corrected his account of the creation, and would have forborne to copy the moral law from the tablets of stone, where it was written with the finger of God, and made his version conform to the earlier and more perfect record. And in that case he would have forborne also, where, afterwards, referring among other things to the announcement of that Law from Sinai, in a voice which shook the earth, to trifle with the Israelites by saying; "Ye shall not add unto the word which I command you, neither shall ye diminish aught from it, that ye may keep the commandments of the Lord your God, which I command you."—Deut. iv.

When a professed believer in the Bible has so much confidence in his inferences from geological facts as to treat the Scriptures in this manner, his example, under the pretence, affectation, and cant of science, falsely so called, is of far worse tendency than that of the unblushing pantheist, at the extreme of human blindness and presumption on the one hand, or that of the dreaming idealist on the other, for they reject the Bible altogether, without attempting to force it to support their theories.

CHAPTER VI.

Notice of Doct. Hitchcock—Religion of Geology

The following extracts from a recent edition of "The Religion of Geology and its connected sciences, by Edward Hitchcock, D.D., LL.D., President of Amherst College and Professor of Natural Theology and Geology," will show that the principal doctrines ascribed to foreign authors, are held at the present time by the ablest and most widely known Geological Author on this side of the Atlantic. These doctrines are put forth as the *science*, or what the science *teaches ;* and on that ground the theologian is expected to modify his interpretation of Scripture, so as to make it at least not inconsistent with the teachings of this *science.*

The present writer is not a little anxious rightly to understand and represent this respected author, and therefore quotes largely from his pages. In his view, the question at issue is a vital one in its relation to the inspired record concerning the creation of the world, its epoch, the reasons of the physical changes which have taken place, the agencies by which they have been effected, the occurrence of successive creations, the reign of death, the extent of the Noachic deluge, and other things treated of in the Holy Scriptures. If he understands Doct. H. correctly, then geology, *as a science*, is to be regarded as a more ancient and more intelligible revelation in respect to these questions, than the text of Scripture; and as furnishing reliable and sufficient data for correcting, modifying, and re-interpreting that text; and therefore that the natural theology which this science teaches must be studied and comprehended first, that its lights may be employed to elucidate, correct, or modify the hitherto received constructions of revelation.

It is manifest that if such claims and pretensions belong to geology as *a science*, then a secondary, inferior, and unauthoritative place must be assigned to the inspired record, so far as these subjects are concerned. But if it is not the science of geology that has any such claims or pretensions, but only the assumptions, hypotheses, and inferences, which the geologists, according to their fancies or preconceived theories, respectively deduce from the physical facts which constitute their science, then the conflict in the case is not a conflict between science and revelation—

the inconsistencies to be reconciled are those only of erring mortals, in conflict with the authoritative, unalterable Word of the Creator and Ruler of the World.

Doctor H. in his work entitled "ELEMENTARY GEOLOGY," defines geology as follows, in the 1st Section :

"*Definition.* Geology is the History of the mineral masses that compose the earth, and of the organic remains which they contain.—*Def.* Every part of the globe, which is not animal or vegetable, including water and air, is regarded as mineral.—*Def.* The term rock, in its popular acceptation, embraces only the solid parts of the globe ; but in geological language, it includes also the loose materials—the soils, clays, and gravels that cover the solid parts—*Stratification.*—*Def.* The rocks which compose the globe, are divided into two great classes ; the STRATIFIED AND UNSTRATIFIED."

Webster defines geology to be "The doctrine or science of the structure of the earth or terraqueous globe, and of the substances which compose it."

The *science* of geology, then, is the *knowledge* of facts respecting the physical substances which compose the globe, and of the physical relations and connections of those substances with one another in the structure of the earth. These facts are to be learnt by observation ; and all that is to be known of them is to be learnt by observation. They are simple, comprehensible, fixed facts. They can be described on paper simply as facts, without any conjectures as to how they were caused, or any inferences as to the time occupied in their causation. The knowledge of them is the science of geology. They are wholly distinct from, and independent of the notions, theories, inferences, conjectures, and hypotheses of geologists or others who observe them. These notions, theories, &c. may be in the utmost degree inconsistent with the plainest statements of revelation, while the facts from which they are pretended to be deduced, may be obviously and demonstrably perfectly consistent with those statements. The geological theories and inferences may proceed upon the assumption that no moral reasons existed for the causation of the facts observed, and that no miraculous or supernatural agency was interposed to cause them, while the facts themselves, from their very nature and relations, considered in connection with the statements of revelation, may clearly indicate that their existence was due wholly to moral reasons and supernatural interference.

Suppose now the geologist to go forth to examine the structure and materials of the globe. He observes two classes of rocks, stratified and unstratified. They are clearly distinguishable. One has a crystallized form and texture, the other such a form and texture as would result from the deposit of mud, sand, and gravel in water. These he calls sedimentary. He finds of these, a regular succession of beds or layers which in the aggregate are some eight or ten miles in thickness. These layers differ from each other in thickness and in their mineral composition; that is, in the kind of earthy materials which they were composed of. He finds them generally tilted up from the horizontal position in which they were deposited, to a greater or less degree of inclination, and sometimes to a vertical position, so as greatly to facilitate his examination of them. He gives distinctive names to these successive layers, indicative of their mineral character, as gneiss, lime-stone, red sandstone, slate, coal, clay, &c. &c. He observes that the lowest of these sedimentary formations everywhere rests on crystalline rock or granite. Again he observes that a large portion of these sedimentary rocks, to the depth of six or seven miles, contains the skeletons and relics of various plants and animals, terrestrial and marine.

Now these and the like undisputed and unquestionable facts constitute what he calls, or ought to call, geology. The observation, study, and knowledge of them constitute the science of geology. The facts exist independently of any theory of causation, or of time occupied in effecting them. They existed ages before geology was studied or heard of. Geology has neither added to nor diminished aught from them, and if geologists had reported them without any of their theories or inferences as to the mode of causation or the lapse of time occupied, no one would have dreamed of their being in any respect in conflict with the Scriptures.

But the geologists, one and all, have occupied themselves mainly in attempting to account for the facts disclosed by their researches upon some theory of the mode in which they were caused, the physical agencies by which they were effected, the time occupied, &c. &c.; and they most unscientifically and unwarrantably denominate the facts, and their theories and inferences conjointly, *the science of Geology.* And inasmuch as their gratuitous theories, assumptions, and inferences, are in many particulars palpably inconsistent with the plain, obvious, natural, and legitimate import of the sacred record, they hesitate not to represent the teachings of their *science* as in conflict with the received, natural, and apparent meaning of the language of revelation. With this view infidelity joins in, forsaking its former haunts as no longer tenable, and takes its refuge, not in the facts of geology, which no one questions, nor in the science founded on those facts, which affords it no hiding-place or security, but in the theories and assumptions of the geologists. Thus, for example, the infidel Lamarckian theory of development is founded on the geological theory of successive creations of plants and animals at successive periods, conformably to the geological theory of the gradual improvement in the condition of the globe under the operation of physical causes, and beginning with the creation of the most imperfect, and rising step by step to those more perfect, till the climax is reached by the production of man. To combat this form and front of infidelity, some of the more recent geological writers abandon, as a false hypothesis, the notion that the products of more recent creations were in any respect more perfect than those which preceded, and aver on the contrary that the earliest were the most perfect, and cite the testimony of the fossil relics in support of this conclusion. Others, however, still adhere to their early and fixed impressions on this and other branches of geological theory.

The work of Doctor Hitchcock now under consideration, comprises fourteen Lectures. Of these, the first is entitled "Revelation illustrated by Science." In this lecture the author states definitely what he apprehends to be "the established principles of the science that have a bearing upon religious truth." Among these, as numerically designated by him, are the following:—2d. The same general laws appear to have always prevailed on the globe, and to have controlled the changes which have taken place upon and within it.—3d. The geological changes which the earth has undergone, and is now undergoing, appear to have been the result of the same agencies, viz. heat and water.—4th. It is demonstrated that the present continents of the globe, with, perhaps, the exception of some of their highest mountains, have for a long period constituted the bottom of the ocean, and have been subsequently either elevated into their present position, or the waters have been drained off from their surface. This is probably the most important principle in geology, and though regarded with much scepticism by many, it is as satisfactorily proved as any principle of physical science, not resting on mathematical demonstration.—5th. The internal parts of the earth are found to possess a very high temperature, nor can it be doubted that at least oceans of melted matter exist beneath the crust, and perhaps even all the deep-seated interior is in a state of fusion.—6th. The fossiliferous rocks, or such as contain animals and plants, are not less than six or seven miles in perpendicular thickness, and are composed of hundreds of alternating layers of different kinds, all of which appear to have been deposited just as rocks are now forming at the bottom of the lakes and seas, and hence their deposition must have occupied an immense period of time. Even if we admit that this deposition went on in particular places much faster than at present, a variety of facts forbids the supposition that this was the general mode of their formation.—8th. Confirmation of the same important principle is found in the well established fact that there have been upon the globe, previous to the existing races, not less than five distinct periods of organized existence; that is, five great groups of animals and plants, so completely independent that no species whatever is found in more than one of them, have lived and successively passed away before the creation of the races that now occupy the surface. Other standard writers make the number of these periods of existence as many as twelve. Comparative anatomy testifies that so unlike in structure were those different groups, that they could not have existed in the same climate, and other external circumstances.—9th. In the earliest times in which animals and plants lived, the climate over the whole globe appears to have been as warm as, or even warmer than, it is now between the tropics. And the slow change from warmer to colder appears to have been the chief cause of the successive destruction of the different races; and new ones were created, better adapted to the altered condition of the globe, and yet each group seems to have occupied the globe through a period of great length, so that we have here another evidence of the vast cycles of duration that must have rolled away, even since the earth became a habitable globe.—10th. There is no small reason to suppose that the globe underwent numerous changes previous to the time when animals were placed upon it; that, in fact, the time was when the whole matter of the earth was in a melted state, and not improbably also even in a gaseous state. These points, indeed, are not as well established as the others that have been mentioned; but, if admitted, they give to the globe an incalculable antiquity.—11th. It appears that the present condition of the earth's crust and surface was of comparatively recent commencement, otherwise the steep flanks of mountains would have ceased to crumble down, and wide oceans would have been filled with alluvial deposits.—12th. Among the thirty thousand species of animals and plants [of which let it be observed, near two-thirds are mollusks and radiated animals] found in the rocks, very few living species have been detected; and even these few occur in the most recent rocks, while in the secondary group, not less than six miles thick, not a single species now on the globe has been discovered. Hence the present races did not exist till after those in the secondary rocks had died. No human remains have been found below those alluvial deposits which are now forming by rivers, lakes, and the ocean. Hence geology infers that man was one of the latest animals that was placed on the globe.—13th. The surface of the earth has undergone an enormous amount of erosion by the action of the ocean, the rivers, and the atmosphere. The ocean has worn away the solid rock in some parts of the world, not less than ten thousand feet in depth, and rivers have cut channels through the hardest strata, hundreds of feet deep and several miles long ; both of which effects demand periods inconceivably long. [Compare this with the 11th principle.]—14th. At a comparatively recent date, northern and southern regions have been swept over and worn down by the joint action of ice and water, the force in general having been directed towards the equator. This is called the drift period.—15th. Since the drift period, the ocean has stood some thousands of feet above its present level in many countries.—16th. There is evidence, in regard to some parts of the world, that the continents are now experiencing slow vertical movements—some places sinking, and others rising. And hence a presumption is derived that, in early times, such changes may have been often repeated, and on a great scale.—17. Every successive change of importance on the earth's surface appears to have been an improvement of its condition, adapting it to beings of a higher organization, and to man at last, the most perfect of all.—Finally. The present races of animals and plants on the globe are, for the most part disposed in groups, occupying particular districts, beyond whose limits the species peculiar to those provinces usually droop and die. The same is true, to some extent, as to the animals and plants found in the rocks; though the much greater uniformity of climate that prevailed in early times, permitted organized beings to take a much wider range than at present; so that the zoological and botanical districts were then probably much wider. But the general conclusion, in respect to living and extinct animals, is, that there must have been several *centres of creation*, from which they emigrated as far as their natures would allow them to range.

"It would be easy to state more principles of geology of considerable importance; but I have now named the principal ones that bear upon the subject of religion. A brief statement of the leading truths of theology, whether natural or revealed, which these principles affect, and on which they cast light, will give an idea of the subjects which I propose to discuss in these lectures.

"The first point relates to the age of the world. For while it has been the usual interpretation of the Mosaic account, that the world was brought into existence nearly at the same time with man and the other existing animals, geology throws back its creation to a period indefinitely, but immeasurably remote. The question is not whether man has existed on the globe longer than the common interpretation of Genesis requires—for here geology and the Bible speak the same language—but whether the globe itself did not exist long before the creation; that is long before the six days' work, so definitely described in the Mosaic account? In other words, is not this a case in which the discoveries of science enable us more accurately to understand the Scriptures?"

Here let us pause and enquire whether the "principles" above recited, in so far as they conflict with the received and obvious interpretation of the Scriptures, are entitled to be called scientific principles, unquestionable facts, or necessary deductions from scientific demonstration, or are of such authority as axioms, intuitions, or facts clearly manifest to observation, as to disprove and nullify the literal and apparent import of the Mosaic account, and render it necessary to reject that account altogether, or by some new interpretation, to reconcile it with the demands of geology? Or whether, on the contrary, whatever in these so-called principles which conflicts with the received interpretation of Scripture, is not mere inference, theory, hypothesis, or conjecture, deduced, or purporting to be deduced, from the facts disclosed by geological research, and, as associated with the real or apparent facts, set forth under the designation of principles, as the teachings, demonstrations, or conclusions of geological science? Do the admitted geological facts (see 6th principle), that the fossiliferous rocks, containing animals and plants, are not less than six or seven miles in perpendicular thickness, that they are composed of hundreds of alternating layers of different kinds, and that all these *appear* to have been deposited, just as rocks are now forming at the bottom of lakes and seas, demonstrate scientifically, unequivocally, and beyond all question, that their deposition occupied an immeasurable period of time? Is not this assumption as to an immense period of time having been so occupied, a mere inference from a prior assumption, that the deposition was caused by the very slow and gradual operation of natural causes? Does the observed and admitted fact that the deposition to the alleged thickness took place, demonstrably prove that it took place by the alleged gradual operation, or how and by what agencies and instrumentalities it was effected; and that there were no moral reasons for a far more rapid process, and for the interposition of supernatural agency? Does the fact that such deposition took place demonstrate that the Creator and Ruler of the world could not possibly have caused it any more rapidly or by any other means than the slow operation of blind, insensate, physical laws? If not, then the science of geology, though it conclusively exhibits the fact that the deposition took place, does not demonstrate that the operation must have occupied an immense period of time, and therefore does not throw the creation back to a point immeasurably distant. The science of geology discloses a stupendous fact respecting the actual structure and condition of the crust of the globe. The geologist imagines and assumes that this existing structure and condition were caused by the slow operation of physical causes, and thence infers that the globe was created at an epoch inconceivably earlier than the "six days," and thereby contradicts the plain import of the inspired account of the creation. The conflict is not that of his science, but that of his inference. The science does not and cannot demonstrate or exhibit any thing to render it even probable that the author of the inspired account, the Creator and Moral Governor of the world, had not moral reasons for his own immediate or supernatural interposition to cause the admitted change in the structure and condition of the fossiliferous and all the sedimentary formations of the globe. And if he had such reasons, then there is nothing in the existing structure and condition of these formations inconsistent or in conflict with his inspired account of the work of creation as having taken place in the six days of the Mosaic narrative.

The inspired account literally and unequivocally asserts that in six days the Lord made heaven and earth, the sea, and all that in them is. It hints at no earlier, or other creation of lands or seas, or living creatures. Does the science of geology then exhibit the indubitable, well established fact (see principle 8th) that there have been upon the globe previous to the existing races, five or more distinct periods of organized existence; five or more great groups of plants and animals, independent of each other, which have lived and successively passed away before the creation of the races that now occupy the surface, and that a change of climate (see 9th principle), caused the successive destruction of the different races; that new races were created, better adapted to the altered condition of the globe, and that each group overspread the globe during periods of such length as to show that vast cycles of duration must have rolled away, even since the earth became habitable? Is not all this sheer matter of hypothesis and inference, from the construction which the geologists put upon the *appearances* of the fossil remains which fall under their observation—appearances, it may be, construed fancifully, or in conformity with some preconceived theory of a scale of being rising from the less to the more perfect, or of an assumed gradual improvement in the condition of the earth by means of the physical changes supposed to have been in progress. And is such an inference entitled to be set forth in opposition to the literal import of the inspired record, as a demonstration of science, with the implied conclusiveness of a mathemetical demonstration? Is the Inspired Word to be modified, explained away, or rejected, to meet the demands of such an inference deduced from such equivocal, uncertain, or merely fancied appearances?

In a word, is any fanciful theory or inference which any geologist of established reputation thinks proper to advance, to be of course taken as a decision or demonstration of science, and as such arrayed against the announcements of Scripture? Is the theory which some geologists hold and others reject, that the whole matter of the earth was once in a melted state, and perhaps even in a gaseous state (see 10th principle), though allowed not to be so well established as some other geologic theories, still, *if admitted*, is it to be taken by those who admit it, in proof of the incalculable antiquity of the globe? Is the extinction of numerous species of plants and animals (see 12th principle), to be taken as conclusive proof that the present races did not exist, till after those which are extinct had passed away? Does geology know for certain when or by what means the lost races were exterminated? If no human remains have been found below the alluvial deposits (see 12th principle), is geology therefore entitled to *infer* and *decide* that man was created ages after those animals whose relics are found further down in the rocks? Is this a demonstration of science, or is it mere conjecture? Is the relative position of those fossil relics which have been discovered, a surer test of chronology than the narrative inspired by the omniscient Creator?

If the science of geology does not in such particulars as those above mentioned, exhibit unquestionable demonstration and indubitable evidence that the common interpretation of the Mosaic account is not true and that the world was in fact created earlier by incalculable ages, and that there have been successive creations, &c; if geology with all its appended theories and inferences, furnishes nothing like positive demonstration or conclusive facts to bring in conflict with the Scriptures, but only assumptions and conjectures which carry an air of plausibility and captivate the imagination, while supernatural interpositions and moral reasons and purposes are kept out of view; then it may well excite our special wonder that the science should be brought into conflict with revelation by any who believe the Scriptures to be inspired. Is it not passing strange that the plain meaning of a record believed to have been dictated by the Creator and Ruler of the world, should be assailed and thrown into doubt, on the ground of a theory of the mode in which physical changes have taken place in the earth? And is it any wonder that when a good man has adopted the geological inferences, and comes to urge them against the received interpretation of Scripture, he should hesitate and feel embarrassed at every step, as one not sure that he is right, where he admits that certainty is of the utmost consequence.

The following extracts are from Doctor Hitchcock's second Lecture, entitled "THE EPOCH OF THE EARTH'S CREATION UNREVEALED." "My simple object at this time is to ascertain whether the Bible fixes the time when the universe was created out of nothing. The prevalent opinion, until recently, has been that we are there taught that the world began to exist on the first of the six days of creation, or about six thousand years ago. Geologists, however, with one voice, declare that their science *indicates* the earth to have been of far higher antiquity. The question becomes, therefore, of deep interest, whether the common interpretation of the Mosaic record is correct." What a falling off! The science, instead of demonstrating or exhibiting indubitable facts to show the earth to be of far higher antiquity than the six days, and thereby furnishing solid ground upon which to call the Mosaic record in question, only *indicates* the earth to have been of that high antiquity; the science, excluding all reference to the miraculous interpositions of the Creator, and the moral reasons announced by him for such interpositions, suggests the possibility, on the ground of analogy in the ordinary operation of physical causes, that the earth may have been of the alleged high antiquity!

The rest of the Lecture seems to be about equally divided in its affirmative and negative suggestions concerning the great question whether the epoch of the earth's creation is revealed or not. After some observations as to "the mode in which the sacred writers describe natural phenomena," the style of the Old Testament, the Scripture usage of the words *created* and *made*, and a citation of the opinions of certain commentators, the author says: "We have only to determine whether the translation of the Mosaic account of the creation *most reasonably* teaches a production of the matter of the universe from nothing, or only its renovation, and we have decided what is taught in the original."

"Now, there can hardly be a doubt but that Moses intended to teach in these passages (the first five verses of Genesis) that the universe owed its origin to Jehovah, and not to the idols of the heathen; and since all acknowledge that other parts of Scripture teach, that, when the world was made, it was produced out of nothing, why should we not conclude that the same truth is taught in this passage? *The language certainly will bear that meaning;* indeed it is almost as strong as language can be to express such a meaning; and does not the passage look like a distinct avowal of this great truth, at the very commencement of the inspired record, in order to refute the opinion, so prevalent in early times, that the world is eternal."

In view of this quotation, it would seem *most reasonable* to conclude that the first five verses of Genesis do reveal the epoch of the production of the matter of the universe out of nothing. For if Moses intended in those verses to teach that the universe owed its origin to Jehovah; if other Scriptures teach that when the world was made it was produced out of nothing; and if the language of these verses, ending with the close of the first day, is almost as strong as language can be to express the idea of the creation of the matter of the universe out of nothing within the compass of those verses, then how can we avoid the conclusion that these verses reveal the epoch of the creation?

But when did that period transpire which ended with the first day? "When," asks Doct. H., "did this stupendous event occur?" The creation out of nothing. "Does the phrase *in the beginning* show us when? Surely not; for no language can be more indefinite as to time."

"It is contended, however, that the first verse is so connected with the six days' work of creation, related in the subsequent verses, that we must understand the phrase *in the beginning* as the commencement of the first day. This is the main point to be examined in relation to the passage, and therefore deserves a careful consideration." Behold now the view taken. "If the first verse *must be understood* as a summary account of the six days' work which follows in detail, then *the beginning* was the commencement of the first day, and of course only about six thousand years ago. But *if it may be understood* as an announcement of the act of creation at some indefinite point in past duration, then a period *may have* intervened between the first creative act and the subsequent six days' work. I contend that the passage admits of either interpretation, without any violence to the language or the narration." Again, "I wish it to be distinctly understood, that I am endeavoring to show only, that the language of Scripture will admit of an indefinite interval between the first creation of matter and the six demiurgic days. I am willing to admit, at least for the sake of argument, that the common interpretation, which makes matter only six thousand years old, *is the most natural.* But I contend that no violence is done to the language by admitting the other interpretation. And in further proof of this position, I appeal to the testimony of distinguished modern theologians and philologists, as I have to several of the ancients. This point cannot, indeed, be settled by the authority of names," &c.

Here then we are left in a state of total uncertainty as to which interpretation is true; and, for aught that appears, are at liberty to adopt one or the other, or neither. We are told that the science of geology teaches, that is—demonstrates, for science does not teach what it does not demonstrate—that the earth was created at an epoch immeasurably earlier than the six days. Then we are told that the inspired narrative of the six days, including the first verse as well as those which succeed, may mean, will bear the construction, nay, most obviously or naturally imports, that the matter of the earth was created out of nothing at the epoch of the six days. Can these alternatives both be true? If not, which shall we reject?

Returning, for one more illustration, to the pre-intimations in the first Lecture of the subjects to be discussed in those which follow, we read: "The introduction of death into the world, and the specific character of that death described in Scripture as the consequence of sin, are the next points where geology touches the subject of religion. Here, too, the general interpretation of Scripture is at variance with *the facts of geology*, which distinctly testify to the occurrence of death among animals, long before the existence of man. Shall geology here, also, be permitted to modify our exposition of the Bible?" Is it so then, that the FACTS of geology indubitably show, or distinctly testify to the occurrence of death among animals long before the existence of man? Is not this assertion a mere begging of the whole question? Is not the alleged existence of animals long before that of man, a mere inference from the *fact* that the fossil relics of animals are found imbedded deep in the rocks, and the assumption that they were so imbedded by the slow operation of natural causes? If they were not imbedded by that slow process, but by a supernatural interposition, then would the author say that they bear any such testimony? Do the *facts* of geology demonstrate that they were not inhumed by miraculous intervention? Would the author for a moment hesitate to speak of the process by which the relics were buried up, as he does in his fourth Lecture concerning the Noachian deluge; where, after stating that "There are reasons, both in natural history and the Scriptures, for supposing that the deluge may not have been universal over the globe, but only over the region inhabited by man," he proceeds—"This is a position of no small importance, and will therefore require our careful examination. And in the beginning, I wish to premise, that *I assume the deluge to have been brought about by natural operations*, or in conformity with the laws of nature. I feel no reluctance in admiting it to have been strictly miraculous, provided the narrative will allow of such a conclusion. *But if it was miraculous, then we must give up the idea of philosophizing about it, and believe the facts simply on the Divine testimony.* For how can we philosophize upon an event that is brought about by the direct efficiency of God ?" Geological philosophizing upon geological facts, is good then only upon the supposition that the facts were caused by the operation of natural laws. If there was any miracle in their production, then the facts may be taken as they are and believed, simply on the testimony of inspiration. Suppose then that the deluge was caused by the miraculous interposition of Divine power, and for the moral reasons assigned in the narrative, and that among the facts produced by that interposition, was that of whelming the animals not preserved in the ark, in the sediment of the dissolved and transported continents, would the facts in that case, respecting the position of the relics of those animals, distinctly testify to the occurrence of their death long before the existence of man ?

CHAPTER VII.

The aversion of geologists to the supposition of Miracles in the production of geological changes—The necessity on their hypothesis of numerous and stupendous miracles—Reference to the theory of Doct. John Pye Smith, of a limited extent of the Deluge—Inexplicable facts of Geology—Pebbles—Coal—"Course of Creation"—Extinction of Races—Preposterous assumptions and inferences of geologists—Their omission of reference to the moral government and purposes of the Creator.

Those geologists who profess to believe the Scriptures, betray a degree of anxiety not to alarm the prejudices of infidels by supposing any miraculous interpositions in the production of those physical results, which they can conceive might, in the course of illimitable rounds of duration, be produced by the operation of physical laws. They seem to have no fear of shocking the infidel by the supposition of things absolutely incredible and impossible, if they are but physical things, and have no relations to a moral government. How far this policy may seem to them to be likely to convert the infidel, and lead him to believe in the

Bible and its numberless miracles, and in the moral government which they attest, they do not tell us; but to us such a course would seem likely to confirm and harden the skeptic in his unbelief, and induce him to think that those who profess to believe the Scriptures have not, after all, any more faith in the miracles of Scriptures than they themselves have.

"I humbly think," says Doct. Pye Smith, "that for the honor of God and the interests of genuine religion, it is our duty to protest against the practice of bringing in miraculous interpositions, to help out the exigencies of arbitrary and fanciful theories." Again: "The Scriptures abundantly show that the Divine Wisdom has not lavished away miracles, but, so far as we know, has wrought them only for the purpose of accrediting the claim of some one who professed to be the bearer of a revelation from God."

Yet when this author was endeavoring to reconcile the first chapter of Genesis with the geological theory of a vastly higher antiquity, he feels no difficulty in supposing that the creation of which Moses gives an account was confined to a small region of the earth; and that "this region was first by atmospheric and geological causes of previous operation under the will of the Almighty, brought into a condition of superficial ruin, or some kind of general disorder"—that is a state of chaos. Now this must have been a miracle if the geological theory is true, and a miracle for another purpose than that of accrediting a prophet. For by that theory the geological causes had, under the will of the Almighty, been during myriads of millions of ages operating to bring the earth forward out of its primeval chaos, and so to improve it as to render it fit for the abode of man ; and if the operation of the same causes under the same will now, by a reverse process, plunged it back into a chaotic state, it must have been by what we call a miracle.

It is of the essence of a miracle to arrest, reverse, or supersede the operation of physical causes, and those causes cannot work opposite results without being reversed by an interposition of power superior to theirs, which is miraculous power. Moreover, if they had during innumerable ages been operating in one direction to improve the earth, they could not suddenly react with such force as to plunge the earth back into a condition of superficial ruin, general disorder, or chaos, without a stupendous miracle, a miracle adequate to undo in a moment the work of untold ages and cycles of duration. And here it may be observed in passing, as one of the long caravan of camels which the geologists find it convenient to swallow, that if the process of sedimentary formations, by wearing down granite rocks, had been going on in every region of the globe for the improvement of its condition during those immeasurable periods of duration, and if a particular region was then brought into a chaotic state, and was by the Mosaic creation remodelled, made, and fitted up for man, it is utterly incredible, not to say impossible, that the re-adjusted region should afterwards present nothing in its geological condition to distinguish it from any other region. That it does not, the geologists doubtless will admit. For if it did, they would have told us long ago where that remodelled and doubly improved region is, and read to us the inscription on its rocks, and shown us wherein its geological characteristics differ from those of other regions, and explained how it happened that the other regions were at the dispersion just as well fitted to be the abode of man as that.

But the author seems to caution us against considering such an interposition as this, a miracle, though rendered necessary to help out the exigency of an arbitrary and fanciful theory, of the six days' work of creation; by asserting that the Divine Wisdom has not lavished away miracles, but has, according to the Scriptures, wrought them only to attest the claim of some one professing to be inspired. Were there then no miracles wrought in connection with the deluge, the declared object and effect of which was, by the power of the Creator over the earth and the seas, to destroy the whole of the human and the inferior races of creatures, except the few preserved by the same power in the ark ? Was there no miracle in the confusion of tongues and dispersion of mankind over the whole face of the earth, the declared purpose of which was to defeat the designs of the builders of Babel ? Can geology account for the origin of the various languages, and the sudden dispersion of man to all parts of the earth, without a real miracle ? Was there no miracle in the destruction of Sodom ? Is it common and matter of ordinary experience, that on occasions of volcanic eruptions which overwhelm adjacent villages, or earthquakes which swallow up cities, or meteoric tempests which burst alike on animal and vegetable life, for the Creator himself to appear visibly on earth, and to forewarn his friends that an overwhelming catastrophe was about to happen, not by the ordinary operations of physical causes, but by his own immediate agency, and for the declared reason that the sin of those to be destroyed was "very grievous," and demanded summary retribution ? Is not the history of the Israelites from the legation of Moses to the death of Joshua, an almost uninterrupted recital of miraculous interpositions, and unsuspended supernatural agency ? Were not the miracles of the pillar of cloud by day and of fire by night, the supply of manna and of water, and others, constant and ceaseless for forty years ? Did the supply of manna, the double supply of it on the sixth day of each week, and omission of it on the seventh day, the supply of quails, the preservation of their shoes and raiment from decay, the passage of the Jordan, the downfall of Jericho, have it for their object to attest the claims of some one professing to be a prophet?

What can we do less than to suppose the venerable author above quoted to be so blinded by his views of the geological theories as to be grievously insensible to the wonders of Divine operation revealed, recorded, and enjoined upon our attention in the Scriptures of truth. He had long been a theological teacher and writer, and a critic of Greek and Hebrew, of no inconsiderable note. Yet he lends himself to the Nebular hypothesis, which never having had a particle of evidence to sustain it, has not any less for being exploded by a telescope. That hypothesis he expounds as follows: "That God originally gave being to the primordial elements of things, the very small number of simple bodies,"—the same, let the reader remember, which the first sentence of the inspired record calls the creation of the heavens and the earth,—"endowing each of those simple bodies with its own wondrous properties. Then, that the action of those properties, in the ways which his wisdom ordained, and which we call laws, *produced, and is still producing, all the forms and changes of organic and inorganic natures;*

and that the series is by Him destined to proceed, in combinations and multiplications ever new, without limit of space or end of duration." That is, as elsewhere taught or implied by him, and more minutely described by other amateurs, the only creation of anything that ever took place, was that of the primordial elements of things. These, in the deep abysses of the past, prior, it must be presumed, to the development of the power of gravitation, were stored up somewhere in a state of igneous fluidity ; ready to be thrown off piecemeal to form suns and planets to be thrust into their several orbits, moulded into their due forms, and subjected to the law of gravitation. The several primordial elements invested with those properties which we call laws, being at length combined, the action of those properties, or laws, began to produce and went on and still go, and are forever to go on producing "all the forms and changes of organic and inorganic natures." If this is not the development theory in all its grossness, it yet would seem to preclude any supernatural interposition in the production of man or of any other creature in the "six days," narrated by Moses.

Again, Doctor Smith, to avoid the supposition of so many miracles as a universal deluge would have required, comes to the conclusion that the Noachic deluge was local and of but limited extent, and that it occurred in the same region where the six days' creation took place. He objects to the universality of the deluge expressly, because it would, in his opinion, have required certain particular miracles which he specifies. A great increase in the quantity of water he supposes would be necessary, and require a miracle. This of course would depend on the height of the mountains. If lofty mountains had not then been forced up, then perhaps no additional quantity of water was needed.

The gathering together of animals, birds, creeping things, and insects from polar, tropical, and all other regions of the earth, to the place where the ark was built, would, he supposes, require "miracles more stupendous than any that are recorded in Scripture." But if the human race had not extended itself beyond the boundary of the *local* deluge, why should the inferior races have spread themselves over the whole face of the globe? The only answer is, the assumption of the geologists, that those races were by successive creations (miracles) brought into existence at different places, which they call centres of creation. But if they were, why not suppose the same of the different tribes of men? By the Scripture account of the "six days," the lower animals and man were created at one time and place. If there were afterwards at other places creations of the lower animals, why not also of man? Who can tell? At best, such successive creations would be miracles, no less than the gathering of specimens of animals created to one place, unless, indeed, those creations were merely the natural effect of physical laws—organic natures produced by the action of the inherent properties of the primordial elements of things, and if so, what should hinder the production of man by force of those properties wherever they were in operation! And in that case what would be the use of a deluge unless it was universal, and such as to be described in the words of Scripture: "*All the high hills that were under the whole heaven were covered. Fifteen cubits upward did the waters prevail: and the mountains were covered. And all flesh died that moved upon the earth, both of fowl and of cattle, and of beast, and of every creeping thing that creepeth upon the earth, and every man: all in whose nostrils was the breath of life, of all that was in the dry land died, and every living substance was destroyed which was upon the face of the ground, both man and cattle, and the creeping things, and the fowl of the heaven; and they were destroyed from the earth; and Noah only remained alive and they that were with him in the ark.*" If it be possible by a multiplication of affirmatives, and details concerning what was or what was not done, to express the idea of unqualified universality, it may safely be deemed to be expressed in these inspired statements. And if the deluge was universal, and was caused, as the narrative attests, by the immediate interposition of the Creator and Moral Governor of the world, for moral reasons which are expressly announced, and which imply the necessity of its being universal, then whatever miracles that interposition produced, must be admitted and believed, or the whole narrative must be given up. The physical difficulties which a creature of the fallen race may conceive of, as to the capacity of the ark to hold all the animals, though expressly constructed under the divine direction for that purpose; as to the provision of suitable food for them; as to marine and fresh water fish living in a mixture of salt and fresh water; and as to the possibility of Noah and the creatures with him descending from the congealed summit of what is now called Mount Ararat; these and all others of the same, or of any other sort, are irrelevant and to no purpose, and cannot, without the utmost impropriety, if the narrative is believed, be adduced in opposition to it.

Let us now see how far the author avoids the necessity of miracles by supposing the deluge to have been limited to that region which at the six days' creation had been brought into a chaotic state, and was remodelled and fitted up for the habitation of man, and which he supposes continued to be his place of abode up to the time of the deluge. In order to make that region the scene of an exterminating deluge of twelvemonths' duration, great physical changes were required in its geological condition. It must be suddenly sunk down after Noah entered the ark so as to hold in the basin thus formed, a sufficient quantity of water. For if the rain of forty days, and the waters of the ocean had been precipitated upon that region while at its former level, the waters would have flowed over adjacent regions, and the deluge would not have been restricted to its proper limits. Accordingly, the author says:— "If in addition to the tremendous rain, *we suppose* an elevation of the bed of the Persian and Indian seas, or a subsidence of the inhabited land towards the south, we shall have sufficient causes, in the hand of Almighty justice, for submerging the district, covering its hills, and destroying all living beings within its limits, except those whom Divine mercy preserved in the ark." Now the sinking of this region at the proper moment, with the ark and all the human and other creatures within the supposed limits, to a depth sufficient to allow the water about to be poured into the basin to cover the high hills of the region, and especially if it included the mountain now called Ararat, with its summit of perpetual ice, would doubtless involve one or more very great miracles, such as may well be referred to the hand of Omnipotence, and if a moral reason for the operation is admitted, to the hand of "Almighty justice." The raising of the bed of the Persian and Indian seas at the same moment, or shortly after, would be necessary in order that their waters might continue to run into the basin till it was full. This would require one or more important miracles. Then a miracle would be required to prevent those elevated seas from running off laterally and submerging other regions of the earth. When the deluge had accomplished its main object, another miracle would be called for to elevate the submerged region to its former level, and another to sink the bed of the Persian and Indian seas again so as to receive back their waters. This, accordingly, the author provides for. "The draining off of the waters would be effected by the return of the bed of the seas to a lower level, or by the elevation of some tracts of land which would leave channels and slopes for the larger part of the water to flow back into the Indian ocean, while the lower part remained a great lake or an inland sea—the Caspian."

It occurs here to observe, that should the geologists ever adopt a theory by which it would be important to discover where the fossil remains of the antediluvians are deposited, they might, following this account of the deluge, be encouraged to look for them under the waters of the Caspian sea, or in its neighborhood.

Such an attempt to substitute a local for an universal deluge, may serve to show how the mind of a geologist, devout and conversant with the Scriptures though he be, may be mystified and bewildered by physical studies, theories, and associations. In no other view is it of any significance or worthy of any respect. If in the Scripture narrative of an universal deluge, any relief in regard to the greatness or number of miracles were needful or desirable, this feigned substitute does not afford it, and in several particulars implies ignorance and foolishness in the inspired account. If the deluge was to be limited to a particular district which comprised all the inhabitants to be destroyed, would it not be folly for Noah to employ himself a hundred and twenty years in forewarning the people of its approach? Would they not feel that they might at a short notice migrate beyond the borders of that district? Would not some living near the borders have time to escape even after the rain began to fall? Could he have produced in any one a conviction that inevitable destruction awaited him in case of the deluge actually happening? And in case of such local deluge, where was the necessity of an ark, and the miracles which it implies whether the deluge was local or universal? Could not Noah, with a hundred and twenty years of prescience, easily migrate with his family and the animals, beyond the foredoomed district?

Geology exhibits to us many remarkable facts which are inexplicable on the current theory, and which we must be content to leave unexplained, or explain by referring them to supernatural agency.

A very large proportion of the "crust" of the earth to the depth of ten miles or more, consists of rocks, clays, &c., formed of sediment precipitated in water; and this vast aggregate of sedimentary matter is distributed into thirty or more distinct layers, differing from each other in their mineral composition.

The distribution of homogeneous mineral matter into the respective layers is, from the nature of the resulting combination, ascribed to chemical action; and it necessarily supposes the presence at the formation of the respective layers, of the *entire mass* of diverse materials out of which, by chemical action, the materials of each particular layer were selected, or else it supposes that the rocks from which, by the geological theory, the sediment was slowly derived, yielded during the formation of the successive layers, only such mineral matter as the layers respectively in their order required. During the vast period therefore, on this latter supposition, occupied in the formation of the lowest sedimentary rock, which rests on the original granite platform, the granite from which the materials were derived by trituration, yielded only that sort of mineral matter which composes gneiss.

Above this, not to mention less important layers, are that of the *primitive* limestone, a thousand feet or more in thickness; the old red sandstone several thousand feet in thickness; chalk a thousand or more feet thick; during the formation of which, respectively, the original unstratified granite rock, the source of sedimentary materials, must have yielded only such mineral matter as each layer while in progress required. Now, if this be not incredible and inconceivable, it would at least be difficult to state a proposition entitled to be so considered. For by the geologic theory of gradual trituration and washing down of the granite rock, each of these layers must have required myriads of ages; and when one layer ceased, and another commenced, the granite must have begun to yield a different mineral matter from that which preceded. If it be said that limestone (and chalk as a carbonate of lime) is formed of marine shells instead of detached and worn down particles of granite, then, during the formation of a bed of limestone rock a thousand feet in thickness, the disintegration and washing down of granite rock must have been suspended till shells enough were produced and aggregated to supply the requisite quantity of materials. But as has been observed before, to suspend the alleged process of detaching and washing down sediment from the granite, would require a stupendous miracle. It would be to suspend the laws of nature over the whole or a large portion of the earth.

It is supposed by the geologists generally, that the interior of the globe—below the crust, which some think may be thirty, and others more than thirty miles thick—is a mass of melted matter. If such is the fact, since it is the nature of heat to rarify and expand the heated matter, one might naturally conclude that the interior would be proportionably lighter than the crust which has been condensed and hardened by cooling. Yet they teach us that as a whole, the earth is about five times heavier than water, and two and a half times heavier than common rocks. Instead therefore of being more rare and expanded than the outer shell, the interior must be far more compact and solid.

The mean depth of the ocean is estimated to be about three miles, while extensive portions of it are supposed to be nine or more miles in depth. The mean height of the land, on the contrary, probably does not exceed a quarter of a mile above the ocean level. The dry land therefore, if spread over the bottom of the ocean, might all be submerged to a considerable depth without any increase in the quantity of water. Yet many geologists, without knowing anything whatever as to the relative height of land and sea at the period of the deluge, object to the universality of that visitation on the ground that there was not water enough to make it universal.

The geologists, in support of the theory of numerous centres of creation in distinct zoological and botanical provinces, allege that very few of the species of plants and animals which they contain, can long survive a removal out of the province where they were originally placed, because their natures cannot long endure the difference of climate, food, and other changes to which they must be subject. Yet they inform us that the carcasses of tropical animals, elephants for example, are found in Siberia, and the remains of tropical plants in the coal formation of Melville Island 75° north latitude.

The theory of "a scale of beings" in which the animals of various species are arranged in a continuous and unbroken series, like the links of a chain, each link in the ascending scale being more perfect than that which preceded it, till man was reached, very naturally furnished the groundwork, or at least a plausible suggestion of the notion, entertained at an early period of geological research, and more or less down to the present day, that the fossil remains of animals were deposited in conformity with such a scale, the most imperfect being lowest down in the rocks, and being in regular order succeeded by more perfect types. From this notion and assumption, resulted the Lamarckian theory of development and the geological theory of successive creations, neither of which can pretend to have even a shadow of plausibility if the assumed order of succession in the fossil relics does not in fact exist. But the progress of observation and research has demonstrated the non-existence of any such succession. Not only is it demonstrated that the fishes and other faunas and the floras of the lowest fossiliferous rocks are as complicated and finished in their structure, and otherwise as perfect as those of any superior group, or those of the present day, but also that the pretended products of successive creations, instead of being deposited in a series separately from each other, are mingled together to such an extent as to take away all support from this source, to the hypothesis of the extinction of species successively to make room for the creation of new ones. [*See Doct. Anderson's work.*]

Pebbles.—From the generally rounded form of pebbles, the geologists treat of them as fragments of rocks, which acquired their globular shape and their smoothness of surface by being rolled in currents of water. Assuming this to be the process, it is obvious to infer from their hardness, the polish which they bear, and the positions in which they are found, that vast periods of time must have been occupied, and an immense amount of friction expended, in their formation. But there are many and very grave objections to the supposition of their having been formed in this manner. An examination of a bed of gravel and pebbles, from a half inch to three or four inches in diameter, will exhibit such a variety in their forms and their mineral composition, as forcibly to suggest the impossibility of their having originally consisted of fragments of rocks, and of their having attained their forms by the friction of rolling in water. The extreme hardness of most of them precludes the supposition that rocks equally hard had been so broken up as to supply the requisite fragments. No known natural process would ever accomplish such a result; and if the fragments were provided, no conceivable amount of rolling and friction against each other, without an extreme vertical pressure, and a motive power far exceeding that of currents of water, would ever wear off their angles and give them their rounded form. Can any one imagine that masses of flint-rock were ever so broken into fragments as to supply the rounded nodules of that mineral; or that rocks of the garnet or topaz family, or any of those of the most simple and homogeneous composition, and of the greatest specific gravity, were ever subjected to such a process; or that if they were they would ever acquire a globular form by trituration in water? Suppose a triangular, flat, or otherwise irregularly shaped fragment of flint-rock to be thrown into a rapid current of water on a rock bottom, or that masses of such fragments were subjected to the action of currents violent enough to drift them, would they roll? An experiment would probably convince any one that they must first be rounded before a tardy or a rapid current of water would give them a rotary motion.

To sustain the popular theory, it would be requisite to show that in chemical or mechanical composition the pebbles are like the rocks from which the supposed fragments were derived. But those fragments were not granite. In their chemical or mechanical structure they are not like granite, or if any of them are, they are but exceptions to a general rule. If the pebbles were formed by rounding the fragments of pre-existing rocks, they must have been such *sedimentary* rocks as their mineral composition in some respects resembles. The pebbles, however, especially the hardest, heaviest, smoothest, and most regularly shaped, are not in their structure *sedimentary*, but either *crystallized*, or their ingredients are mechanically combined otherwise than in sedimentary rocks. In general, they exhibit the appearance of having been chemically or mechanically formed in the beds which they now occupy, after the mineral matter of which they consist had been accumulated in those beds ; and their position, in relation to the clay, sand, chalk, or other materials by which they are surrounded, cannot be satisfactorily accounted for on any other supposition. They are aggregations of quartz, feldspar, mica, or other simple homogeneous matter, chemically and mechanically separated from the earthy mass around them ; and owing their spherical, oblong, prismatic, or other forms and their smooth surfaces, to the same laws to which diamonds and other crystals owe their peculiar forms and polished sides. Flint pebbles abound in chalk-beds, where they could scarcely have been deposited by currents of water ; for when, if ever, they were diffused and deposited in their present state at all levels, the chalk must have been in so soft and movable a condition as to offer no resistance to such currents. Moreover, they, like many other pebbles in wholly different situations, when broken often exhibit at the centre a nucleus of the aggregation, which cannot be supposed to have existed in the centre of broken fragments of pre-existing rocks, rounded by attrition, and then floated to their permanent position as pebbles.

The theory of rounding by attrition is incompatible with the variety of forms of the existing pebbles. Many of them are thin, with two flat and smooth surfaces, and a circular, elliptical, or other regular curvilinear periphery. No one surely can imagine that such forms, equally polished throughout, could be produced by rolling, or any other possible motion in water. Many of them likewise are oblong, egg-shaped, and differing in every conceivable degree from exact spheres, and yet equally smooth on every portion of their surface. In numerous instances those which are extremely hard lie side by side with others of no more solidity than indurated clay or soft red sandstone, which, if subjected to such action of water as would abrade and change the forms of the harder specimens, would be instantly destroyed. And again, in the same gravel-bed, and in immediate contact with each other, are scores of pebbles differing in their mineral composition as widely as pure silex differs from mica or any compounded mineral.

These and other obvious difficulties attending the prevalent theory, besides those which relate to the transportation and deposition of the rounded pebbles to the positions which they occupy in loose gravel-beds, and in conglomerate rocks, and breccias, are avoided by the supposition of their having been formed by chemical and mechanical forces of comminuted sedimentary matter in the beds in which they now exist. And why should they not owe their consolidation, the ingredients of which they respectively consist, their peculiar forms, and their regular and polished surfaces, to those forces under appropriate circumstances, as truly as the rocks under other circumstances from which, by the common theory, fragments were detached to be rounded into those forms? or as the topazes, the cornelians, the sapphires, hyacinths, rubies, emeralds, beryls, or any of the numerous families of crystallized minerals? Will not the same chemical affinities and mechanical combinations account for the selection of mineral substances, the forms assumed, and the smooth and glass-like surfaces, in the one case as well as in the other?

Without a more extended or minute elucidation of this subject, the foregoing observations may suffice to show that the geologic theory concerning pebbles is untenable; that it involves difficulties which it cannot obviate; that it is assumed, not proved; and that no just inference can be deduced from it in support of preadamite cycles of duration. The same natural causes to which the geologists ascribe the formation of rocks in extended masses, were adequate to the formation of pebbles out of similar materials; and no reason can be assigned why those causes should not have operated in the latter as well as in the former of these instances.

Coal.—The following extracts concerning the coal formation, are taken from the recent work of John

Anderson, D.D., of Scotland, entitled "The Course of Creation." [See chap. 5, *Time and the Geological Epochs.*]

"The carboniferous class of rocks have all the marks of a very peculiar formation, constructed for a special purpose, and elaborated amidst an extraordinary state of things. Here we meet with vast accumulations of vegetable, calcareous, and metallic substances, for which we detect no anterior preparations. The coming on and the outgoing of the whole coal series are as distinct as they are surprising. To what are we to compare them? By what scale of time are we to adjust the terms of their growth?" After referring to calculations that have been made as to the rate of increase per annum of pure vegetable matter over a given area, he gives as the result, "That about six hundred thousand years were occupied in the production of the whole coal series." But this calculation of time proceeds upon two assumptions: 1st. That the volcanic and other violent forces supposed to have been in operation in preceding periods, were suspended during the period of extraordinary vegetable growths, so that "throughout the whole of the carboniferous era a state of repose seems to have universally prevailed." 2d. That "all the living productive powers of nature were just as violently in operation as the others were quiescent," and that a condition of nature existed, " that produced uniformity of vegetation over the entire surface of the globe, as the coal deposit everywhere manifests, and all of gigantic dimensions in every family of plants—the whole earth being covered with a flora not only of unrivalled exuberance, but of uniform distribution nearly on every part of its surface."

Now suppose these conditions to have existed, and the crust of the globe to have been kept in a state of repose for six hundred thousand years, after the upheavals, agitations, and tempests of the preceding ages, whence and by what means were the earthy materials, the rocks and shales provided, which rest on the coal, and are interposed between successive beds of that mineral? That vast masses of those materials must have been universally at hand, and in a condition to be rapidly moved and universally diffused in water, and precipitated on the accumulated vegetable matter, is manifest. This the author admits, and cites in proof of it the frequent occurrence of " fossil trees in the coal measures in an upright position, or but little inclined to the plane of stratification. These are numerous," he adds, " in every coal field, and are often traced through several layers or beds of rock. The fossil trees of Craigleith and Granton were about fifty feet in length, and lying at an angle of scarcely twenty degrees to the strata in which they are imbedded. Their passage through the solid rock, therefore, cannot be estimated at less than fifteen to twenty feet, that is, a mass of sandstone of corresponding depth must have been formed during the comparatively short period that trees of lofty stature were able to resist the destroying action of the elements, to say nothing of the chances of currents, hurricanes, and other agents, breaking them in pieces. This *instantia crucis* may be extended to every sandstone bed of the formation, and thus serve to exercise a salutary restraint upon the mind in its imaginary conceptions of the enormous periods of time required for the accumulation of the whole series."

But though this author is thus convinced that the process of sedimentary deposit must, in the case referred to, have been very rapid, if not instantaneous, universally, he suggests no resource of sedimentary matter universally present to be thus quickly deposited, no mode in which it could be universally and rapidly diffused in water, no means by which only homogeneous materials should be furnished, nor any evidence that successive coal-beds were formed by successive vegetable growths on the successive overlying beds of rock. The whole process, as conceived of by him, may safely be pronounced impossible. From the universality and simultaneousness of the formation, as represented by him, it follows that the vegetable growths occurred within the areas which they now occupy in the form of coal. They could not have been transported from a distance without precluding so general a deposit of coal. The successive layers could not have been produced by growths on the rocks on which they now rest, for those rocks exhibit no traces of soil between their surfaces and the coal itself. During the progress of those growths the area which they occupied could not have been overflowed with water; and when advanced to maturity, nothing short of an universal deluge would account for their being simultaneously submerged and covered with sediment.

The assumed period of repose is not sufficient to account for any item of the whole process, unless it be the supposed universal exuberance of vegetation; and that would imply a state of the earth altogether more perfect than it has exhibited at any more recent period, or does at present, and which at least is not very likely to have been interposed between the previously unbroken series of convulsions, and the ensuing period, of which the author says: "The carboniferous period was immediately succeeded by a period of great violence and of vast disturbance in the solid crust of the earth. Hence the broken, inclined position of the coal strata," &c.

Many at least of the insurmountable difficulties of this theory may be avoided by supposing that no preceding ages of convulsion took place; that the earth was created with a surface not of barren rocks, morasses, and sandy deserts, but complete and perfect in all its adaptations, and universally prepared to be spontaneously and most exuberantly prolific of vegetable growths; that in the course of 1600 years it became stocked with a sufficient quantity of such growths to supply all the vegetable deposits of the coal measures; that in consequence of the apostasy and wickedness of man it was then destroyed by the waters of the deluge, its animal and vegetable races submerged, and its prolific soil diffused in the waters, and by chemical and other agencies separated and distributed into homogeneous layers in a regular and conformable series; that it was afterwards subjected to volcanic and other convulsions, its mountain ranges elevated and bearing upon their summits the sedimentary rocks by which they were previously overlaid, its stratified formations elsewhere tilted and contorted as the geologist now finds them, and its carboniferous, mineral, and metallic treasures, thereby rendered accessible to the toil of degenerate man, and subservient to the wants of his shortened and precarious life.

For this course of things there was a moral reason; a reason connected with those facts of man's early history, his moral defection and physical degradation, of which, in their exhaustless hereditary virulence and misery, we ourselves are witnesses and monuments ; a reason, connected with all the subsequent dispensations and measures of Providence and grace, down to the consummation and restitution of all things ; a reason, intrinsically and in all its bearings and relations, adequate and worthy to be announced by the Creator and moral governor of the universe.

But for the other course of things—the fancied course of successive creations and extinctions, turbulence and repose, doing and undoing, with at best none but physical reasons, or rather the blind, insensate tendency and operations of physical laws, as a guide, what have the geologists to say for it? Why, that the planet as originally created was a shapeless mass of discordant materials, left to be nursed up by the discipline of earthquakes, volcanoes, tempests, cataclysms, and successive creations, destructions, and re-creations, till, on reaching its present state of improvement, it was fit to be inhabited by men, notwithstanding that the greater part of its surface still consisted of barren deserts, congealed artics and inaccessible mountains. Countless myriads of ages having been occupied in this process of improvement, the "Course of Creation" ceased, the measure of perfection had been attained. The production of man was the climax : Some at least holding that no subsequent act of creation has taken place ; while others talk as familiarly of new creations of plants and animals, as new centres of creation invite them, as they talk of such operations in relation to the immeasurable past.

In this course of things one gifted, practised, Christian man, a lay-theologian, writer, and editor, of the Free Church of Scotland, discerns "The Foot-prints of the Creator"—the foot-prints of the Being of Infinite perfection, who spake and the heavens and earth existed, as the theatre of His moral and spiritual empire, the scene of his boundless and endless administration in the disclosure and manifestation of himself to His intelligent creatures; and in comparison with whose physical works, this planet is but as a small particle of dust.

Another not less gifted and Christian man, of the same country, a Doctor of Theology, discerns in this progress of things "The Course of Creation,"—as if that glorious Being, with all His moral purposes and manifestations in abeyance, had employed Himself millions of ages in bringing this particle of dust into a habitable condition, though an instant volition would have endowed it with a completeness worthy of His own perfection: as if He had successively exerted innumerable acts of creation, only to be nullified by corresponding exterminations: and at last produced only such a world of chaotic disorder as the geologists report this to be, and such a scene of life taken as a whole, as is barely tolerable to a fallen race ; a world which yet requires a physical renovation to fit it for the race when renovated and restored to their original state as moral beings.

Of Doctor Anderson, however, whose work has been received only since these sheets were placed in the hands of the publisher, and of which, therefore, only a very slight inspection has been practicable, it may be proper to say, that he seems less under the spell of geologic infatuation than his contemporaries, and especially in respect to what he terms *the millionade doctrine ;* the untold, incalculable, and inconceivable myriads of millions of years, which, absurd as the supposition of them is, are yet absolutely indispensable to the *scientific* theory of geologic causation. Though he holds to a far higher antiquity of the earth than of man, he all but ridicules the excessively prodigal use of such terms as myriads and millions to account for what he deems more likely to have been produced in thousands or scores of thousands of years. " As to the *millionade doctrine*, if I may so term it, there are in every view the greatest difficulties in the way of its adoption—errors of calculation somewhere to be corrected, inconsistencies to be reconciled, conditions of organic life gratuitously assumed and to be rectified. It matters not, indeed, whether we take the organic or the inorganic structures of the several periods as the gauge of their probable duration—the living tribes that existed throughout such periods, and whose relative ages we can approximate to—or the dead rock in which the remains are interred. The Laws of Nature, in the one case, are nearly uniform; species as well as individuals, have their limited terms of existence; and experience establishes the fact that the living tribes of the modern epoch have, in several instances, become extinct within a comparatively short period of time. The operations of nature in the other case are subject to vast diversity, great and sudden changes, and apparently limited by no ascertained maximum of development, and thus combined, so far as our present state of knowledge extends, the inference is warrantable, that in the geological register the error may be one of MILLIONS of years reckoning!"

Nevertheless this sedate, instructed, and thoughtful writer is in doubt concerning the "six days." He speculates upon them under different aspects and with reference to different theories. "If any departure from the literal rendering of the text can be permitted, so as to fit in and adjust the geological phenomena, it may be justly contended that there is less of violence and straining by the substitution of *periods* for *days*, than by casting aside the whole genetic description as having no bearing whatever upon the primary cosmogony of the globe." After noticing several modes of reconciling the Mosaic text with the geologic phenomena, without seeming to adopt or to be satisfied with any of them, he says, "There is still a great deal to be accomplished, even with all these approximations, towards a right and full and literal comparison with the same text. It is better, infinitely better, to rest with unhesitating confidence in the received interpretation of Scripture, than be borne away by sweeping generalizations, built most certainly somewhere upon loose, conflicting elements of calculation. Countless millions of years are, we admit, as nothing in the records of eternity, of no account with the Everlasting of days. Nevertheless, if the time can be reduced, as unquestionably there are data for the reduction, the epoch and the days approximate all the closer; the speculations of the science are brought into better keeping with the dicta of revelation; farther discoveries will lead to farther adjustments; and what was done for the interests of the one by detecting the miscalculations of Hindoo astronomy, will again be effected for the other by scanning more intelligibly the geological horoscope—and thus removing every ground of suspicion or offence will serve to bring this interesting branch of knowledge from the outer court of the Gentiles to the innermost shrine of the TEMPLE OF TRUTH."—*Chap. 6th.*

Had it occurred to this inquisitive and candid author

before he commenced his geological researches, or when he began the composition of his work, that all the leading facts of geology are far more easily and credibly to be accounted for by ascribing them to the immediate and summary interposition of the Creator and Moral Governor of the world by means of the Noachic deluge and its attendant phenomena; for the reason assigned for that stupendous and world-wide visitation; and by the use of the materials, the mineral matter, the vegetation, and the animal organisms of a previously perfect condition of the earth, its prolific soils, its climates and its spontaneity; than by any of the theories of insensate laws with whatever liberty of unlimited drafts upon time, it may be presumed to be not improbable that he would have come to the unwavering conclusion that the received literal import of the Mosaic record is that which the inspiring Spirit intended to convey.

Extinction of Species of Plants and Animals.—In the fossiliferous groups of rocks are found the relics of various extinct species of plants and animals; and it is very obvious to ask, on supposition that those species were created at the Mosaic epoch, and that their relics have since been fossilized, how and why they have become extinct? The geologic theory assumes that they were created at successive periods, long anterior to the Mosaic epoch, as the earth became fitted to be their abode, and that the products of each creation were exterminated to give place to their successors. On that hypothesis, it would, contrary to the fact, be natural to expect that none of the fossilized species would be reproduced in succeeding, and especially in the latest or Mosaic work of creation. If they were all created at the Mosaic epoch, and have since become extinct, the mode of their extinction may, perhaps, be undiscoverable by us; but the reasons for it, we may safely conclude to have been the same as those for shortening man's life, and for the various physical changes the earth has undergone. There were moral reasons for great physical changes in the earth and its climates, its productions and adaptations in all respects to be the scene of life, at the era of the deluge; as is evident from the announced and the observed results. That the extinction of many species of plants and animals should be among these results, is not less credible than that an abridgment of eighty or ninety per cent. of the years of man's life should be among them. Suppose the only creation of plants and animals to have been that of the "six days," and that specimens of every species were preserved in the ark, all the rest of all the species being destroyed and their relics buried; and suppose that on emerging from the ark, the changed condition of the earth from extreme fertility to extreme barrenness, precluded the continued existence of many species of herbivorous animals, and thence precluded the continued existence of many of the carnivorous species; and that those of different species which escaped were favored, some by the foresight and care of man, and others by climate, local position, peculiar habits, or other circumstances; would not such a condition and course of things sufficiently account for the result in question,—the extinction of species? Suppose again, what is neither incredible nor improbable, that among the changes effected in connection with the deluge, the polar axis of the earth was changed from a horizontal direction at right angles with the plane of the equator, to its present inclined direction, causing a change in the now temperate and frigid zones, from equatorial warmth to the perpetual congelation of the polar circles, and the extremes and vicissitudes of the more temperate latitudes. The considerations in favor of such a change, it is not now necessary to adduce. The change was as practicable, and in itself as likely to be effected, as that, or any of those, which caused terrene sterility, and abridged the life of man. It cannot be demonstrated that such a change took place, neither can the contrary be demonstrated. If it took place, it affords a further solution of the extinction of species, and throws some light on one of the stumbling-blocks of geology, viz. the existence of the relics of tropical plants and animals in the frigid and polar regions.

Were then, it may be asked, the extinguished species of animals preserved in the ark, only to perish by famine and by insupportable climates, on emerging from it? Such a question may be fitly answered by another. Did man enter the ark with a constitution of nine hundred years' duration, and quit it only to propagate a diseased and puny race, a small portion only of whom withstand the physical evils within and around them, so long as seventy years? Did not the tribes of giants, the sons of Anak, the denizens of Bashan and of Gath, become extinct, as well as the megatheriums of Zoology? Is it not notorious, and among the things admitted and alleged by geologists of the greatest name. 1st, That, including the whole period of organized existence, the same genera and species of plants and animals have been common to the four quarters of the globe. 2d, That the fossil remains of plants and animals entombed from the beginning to the end of the pretended inconceivable cycles of time, are the remains only of a few great families. 3d, That in all the pretended new creations of plants and animals in the progress of the great geologic periods, no new types, no individuals even, but those of preceding genera and species have been produced. 4th, That the most ancient fossil remains, that is, those farthest down in the rocks, of plants, insects, mollusks, fishes, reptiles, birds, and beasts, are as perfect in their several kinds as their survivors of the present day: And 5th, That whole genera and species, as well as individuals of plants and animals, which survived the fossiliferous period, have become extinct within the modern period of physical and civil history?

That there are facts disclosed by geological research which, in certain relations, are utterly inexplicable to us, no one who has the slightest knowledge of the subject can hesitate to acknowledge—facts which it is neither within the province of science nor of Scripture to explain. But they are, as facts relating to physical phenomena, not in themselves more wonderful or more inscrutable, than other facts which relate solely to moral and spiritual phenomena. A natural philosopher, excluding from his view the records of inspiration, can no more explain or account for the facts of the moral world, than the same philosopher, shutting his eyes to all but the lights of science, can explain or account for the facts of the physical world. The two sets of facts are, in original and manifold relations, so involved with each other, that neither can be explained separately. The reason why the Creator governs the physical world by a method of general laws, mechanical, chemical, &c., was not that such laws were necessary either to the existence or the government of physical nature. They are not properties of matter, for if they were, each of them would necessarily be common to all the rest. There could be no diversity of effects, nor indeed any changes, or any chemistry. The force of each property would, in relation to the others, be the same under all conditions. The effect of a contact of oxygen with any other property would be the same as that of contact with carbon. They are not of the nature of matter. They are but the rules and method of his efficiency ; and the reason of them, and of their being just what they are, in respect to their uniformity, universality, and force, lies in the high moral purposes and ends for which He created and governs the world.

The assumption, which appears to have the most powerful and extensive influence on the minds of geologists in leading them to adopt their theory of the high antiquity of the globe, is that the sedimentary masses were formed, and their fossil relics buried, by the ordinary operation of the laws of matter. Physical science exhibits to their observation no other causes. In reasoning about the results, they regard them as the only causes. They exclude from their view all supernatural interference. They leave out of their consideration the moral government of the Creator, and the moral reasons and purposes which He assigns for creating the world and interposing to change its physical condition. However much they may regard those things in other relations, they do not belong to their science, or to their field of research as geologists; and the whole difficulty in relation to the narratives inspired by the Creator, arises not from the facts of geology in themselves, but wholly from the restricted scientific view of them considered as having been caused by mere natural physical properties or laws, which the geologists take, and the inferences which they deduce from these views.

Doubtless, no rational creature can behold the vast masses of sedimentary matter, which to a great depth constitute the crust of the globe, or inspect in detail the wonders which they exhibit, and believe at the same time that the whole of those masses with their fossil contents, were deposited by the slow, uniform, unaided, operation of physical laws, without inferring at once that the process must have occupied immeasurable periods of duration. But before he can make that inference, and as the sole ground of it, he must first assume that those sedimentary masses were formed by the physical causes and in the manner represented. Of that assumption, however, he can adduce no positive evidence whatever; nor anything but an inference from the fact, that at present the operation of those causes is slow, uniform, and unaided: and he therefore infers that it always was so. An admission that for moral reasons, a different, a supernatural process, may have been interposed by the Creator and moral governor of the world, would preclude his inference, and destroy the basis of his main assumption, and of the theory founded on it.

But waiving such admission of moral reasons and supernatural operations, he clings to his main assumption, and makes it the basis of various other assumptions involved in his theory: Such as, that if the formation of the sedimentary masses occupied an immeasurable tract of ages, their object must have been to improve the condition of the planet and render it habitable; that the earth, therefore, must originally have been in a most imperfect condition; that, according to the theory of some, it was in a state of igneous fluidity; and according to others, that it was a shapeless mass of nebular matter; that since none of these things could possibly be true, if the heavens, the earth, the sea, and all that in them is, were created, and created perfect in the space of six days, at the Mosaic epoch; therefore, they were not created at that epoch; that the first verse of Genesis, therefore, does not belong to the narrative of the six days; that the work of those six days was not a creation, but a special fitting up of the whole or a part of the earth; that the Sabbath, therefore, was not instituted as a sign, memorial, or periodical public acknowledgment and attestation that in six days the Jehovah made the heavens and earth, the sea and all that in them is, but was instituted for some other purpose.

None of these assumptions admit of any positive evidence, whether taken separately or collectively; and they are, one and all, utterly baseless and preposterous, unless the main assumption at their head is unequivocally admitted.

We are entitled, therefore, when told that the science of geology is in conflict with revelation, to deny it, and to reply, that it is not the science, its facts, or any legitimate inductions from them, but only the gratuitous assumptions of the geologists that are in such conflict. It would be as legitimate to infer, as some do, from the facts of geology, that the earth was eternal, as to infer that the physical laws or properties of matter, were exclusively the cause of those facts.

The geologists, while they take the liberty to make quite free with the text of Scripture, and with its miracles, as appears from the specimens of their expositions heretofore quoted,—complain loudly of those who call their theories in question, on the ground that they are not practical geologists, and, therefore, cannot be qualified to perform the office of objectors: as if a practical knowledge of facts and details which they do not dispute, would be of any use to enable them to controvert what they do dispute. They are especially impatient of theological assailants, for reasoning from a non-geological book, and arraying moral facts and revealed doctrines against their hypothetical inferences. They forget that the doctrines of Revelation, and the inferences deduced from the facts of the moral world, are far more certain, and of far higher authority than the theories inferred from the phenomena of the physical world. And they likewise seem to forget that in so far as there are known and adequate moral reasons for any physical phenomena, diverse from the geologic reasons, the bearing of those moral reasons may be urged with as much propriety by one who has not, as by one who has devoted his life to the study of geology. It is not against geological facts that such opposition will array itself, but only against preposterous, unscientific, and unscriptural assumptions and inferences from those facts. The facts are not denied or doubted. It is the causes of the facts, or the mode and object of their causation, that challenges enquiry and dissent. Were the geologists content with what strictly belongs to their science, the study and arrangement of geologic facts with their observed connections and relations, no one would have cause to find fault with them, or to diminish aught from the admiration due to their mental and physical labors, their diligence, their perseverance, their achievements, and their fame.

But geology is not everything. It has comparatively but a narrow and limited province. Its progress as a science has been abundantly rapid; but it is not yet old or mature enough to assume to sway its fossil trident over the realms of matter, and also over the domains of life, and the empire of moral and spiritual natures, causes, agencies, and events. Other subjects and provinces of knowledge there are, which have been longer studied and are better settled than geology can claim to be; and which are not to be unceremoniously motioned aside, and treated as old wives' fables, by that young aspirant, armed though he be with fossil bones, and shielded by the mask of a preternatural antiquity.

CHAPTER VIII.

The Theory of the Creation, at first, of only the Primordial Elements of things, considered.

At present it is a favorite notion with many geologists which they employ in aid of their hypothesis concerning the remote epoch of creation, that only the *primordial elements* of matter were at first produced. The creation of the heavens and earth announced in the first verse of Genesis, they suppose to have been a creation only of those elements, and since those elements cannot act each separately upon itself, nor any two of them upon each other until they are brought into contact, their existence separately at first, would form a very suitable starting point of a theory of changes, developments, progress, and improvement, when they were brought into the necessary contact and relations, as the moulding of the earth into an oblate spheroid, the formation of its crust and the subsequent provision and arrangement of its sedimentary matter, gave occasion. That all this progress and these changes, should be the result of the chemical properties originally inherent, though dormant, in the separate elements; and that the physical world as it now is, has in this manner come to be what it is, seems to many to be a very beautiful notion, and worthy to excite our special wonder and admiration at the works of nature. Those elements are now everywhere combined in the physical substances within our observation. But chemistry shows us that they may be separated and resolved into their single and dormant condition as elements; and hence the most simple idea of a creation is that of a production of these elements uncombined. And this idea is thought to be philosophical; it being assumed that when combined or brought into contact in their proper relations, they would operate all the results exhibited in the phenomena of the earth.

Whether any chemical process has as yet reached the last analysis of any one of those elements, no one can tell. If not, the heavens and the earth may at first, according to this hypothesis, have consisted only of gases a thousand times more subtle than any hitherto detected; and by the same rule, the more subtle, the more simple the idea of their creation. How they first began to come into contact so as to act upon each other and set on foot the career of improvement, the theory does not explain. But it is easy to imagine that a vast length of time would be required to bring the earth into a solid, ponderable, and useful form.

If this was the mode of creation, and all organic and inorganic natures are the products of this chemistry, then when we read in the narrative of the "six days" that the Creator said "*Let there be light, and there was light,*" we are to understand that these primordial elements, having been created long before, were now brought into contact, co-action, or combination so as to constitute light. And where it is said, "That God created great whales and every living creature that moveth in the waters—and every winged fowl after his kind—and made the beast of the earth after his kind, and cattle after their kind, and every creeping thing after his kind—and created man in his own image—and made every plant of the field before it was in the earth—and in the day that the Lord God made *the earth and the heavens;*" we must understand that he created the primordial elements of those organic natures at the indefinitely remote epoch prior to the six days which is assumed to be referred to in the first verse. From that epoch they existed in thesi. The great laboratory of elements having in the mean time condensed and moulded the planet into its globular form and generated tempests from above and beneath, to change, distort, and improve, and fit it up for such creatures, they accordingly in the "six days" of Moses burst forth into life. Simple, beautiful process of Nature; requiring no perplexing references to moral natures, reasons, purposes, or government; requiring no providence but that of the general laws, properties, or tendencies inherent in the primary elements, and worthy to be the invention of fallen man.

Now let it be considered that these primordial elements, supposing them to have been created separately or uncombined, could not by the laws which science recognizes as governing them, produce any mechanical or chemical action upon each other, or operate any results whatever, except as those of them which were capable of mechanical combination, or had a chemical affinity for each other, were brought into contact under certain conditions.

If they were created separately and uncombined, then they might have continued to exist separately, and have maintained in their dormant state the same proportions of quantity to each other which they now possess.

In that case when they began to come into contact, and to act on each other, what was it that determined the proportions in which they should unite? Not the laws themselves by which they mechanically or chemically combine when brought together. It is the province of those laws merely to work the effect of contact, not to regulate the proportions or quantities of elements coming together. All beyond the mere physical effect of contact must be owing to an extraneous cause.

In the composition of the atmosphere, for example, how happens it that oxygen and nitrogen are united in the proportions of twenty-one to seventy-nine ? Science can show that in respect to their relative quantities, these proportions exist on the highest mountains as well as near the earth, but it is not in the laws which govern these elements to determine these or any other proportions. The two elements may be entirely separated, and they may be united in any other proportions. Undoubtedly, if united in any other relative proportions they would not constitute an atmosphere fit for respiration, or for that chemical operation by which the life and growth of plants is carried on. But still the fact of their existing in the atmosphere in those proportions is in no degree due to the laws inherent in them, but considered in relation to those laws, is a supernatural fact, a miracle. The primordial elements, had they been created separately, and then left to themselves, would have remained forever separate. Left to themselves, notwithstanding their inherent powers or capabilities of reciprocal action, they would never have united, either in right proportions or in any proportions. To suppose the contrary is to suppose them endowed with vitality and intelligence. A power as foreign and as superior to them as that by which they were created, would be necessary to bring them into those adjustments and relations with each other which would be necessary to produce such results as actually appear in the existing phenomena of the earth and its atmosphere. That is, a constant miracle, equal to that of the creation, or rather an infinite variety of constant miracles would be necessary to render the earth habitable and continue it so. Is it owing to a conviction of this that the geologists, with all their knowledge of chemistry, botany, zoology, mineralogy, and other sciences, and notwithstanding the confidence with which they teach us how the sedimentary masses were formed, and how their materials were derived from crystalline rocks, have none of them attempted to show how, either the atmosphere or the salt waters of the ocean, or the fresh waters of the earth were constituted of the primordial elements into which they are severally resolvable? or where those primordial elements previously existed?

Experimental chemistry has distinguished about fifty-five elementary or undecomposed substances, or modifications of matter. About half of these are designated as metallic, and the other half as non-metallic. The two classes have, under appropriate circumstances or adjustments, a chemical affinity for each other, which is more or less realized and noticeable in all instances of combination in the earth, and in all instances of organization in plants and animals. There is, however, a vast inequality in the distribution of them. Some eight or ten of them constitute the bulk of the atmosphere, the earth, and all plants and animals. The atmosphere is made up of two of them, oxygen and nitrogen; with a trace or comparatively small portion only of two others, carbon and hydrogen, the carbon being in proportion to the whole as one to two thousand, and the hydrogen or vapor of water varying in quantity with the temperature.

These constituents of the atmosphere are mechanically mingled, not chemically combined. When one of the most, and one of the least abundant of them, oxygen and hydrogen, are chemically combined they constitute water; and in this form they occupy about three fourths of the surface of the globe.

The solid earth is chiefly made up of the oxides of one non-metallic body, silicum; and two metals, aluminium, and calcium the metallic base of lime. Add to these potassium, sodium, and iron, and we have all the known components of the earth which enter in considerable quantities into its composition. Sulphur, magnesium, and some others exist in local deposits here and there; while a large number of the elementary bodies are to be found only in rare minerals, or so sparsely diffused as barely to be detected.

In the organic world, the four elements which constitute the atmosphere, are the principal; besides which there is a minute proportion of phosphorus and of sulphur, and a still less proportion of two or three alkalies and earthy salts; the combination of the whole being chemical.

Substances possessing properties of the most diverse and opposite kind, are made up of the same elementary materials; as sugar and vinegar, for example, from carbon, hydrogen, and oxygen, slightly differing in the proportions in which they are combined. Bread is nutritious and healthful, owing to a combination in due proportions of the same elements, which, combined in other proportions, produce the poisonous juice of the poppy. The slightest difference in the relative proportions of the elements of which such compounds consist, may occasion widely various results.

Suppose then the primordial elements to have been created separately, and ready for the operation of the laws mechanical and chemical, which govern their various mixtures and combinations. It is palpable that those laws do not in any degree control the circumstances or conditions under which they shall be adjusted to each other so as to unite mechanically or chemically, nor the proportions of different elements which shall under any given circumstances be brought into the requisite contact or relation. If brought into the necessary relation by gravitation or motion, or by any physical cause, their proportions of quantity to each other would still be undetermined and uncontrolled.

In the atmosphere, for instance, the due composition of which in respect to the relative proportions of its elements, is equally essential to the existence of plants and animals; a different relative quantity of the respective elements, or a different mode of mixture, would have been fatal. Had the whole quantity of the respective elements been the same as now, yet if the relatively small quantity of carbonic acid had not been equally diffused, the result would not have been such an atmosphere as we now possess. The two leading elements, oxygen and nitrogen, are specifically lighter than carbon, and had gravitation controlled the position of the latter element in its relation to the others, it would have formed a stratum by itself, of poisonous, irrespirable gas, on the surface of the earth, to the height of about thirteen feet. Again, nitrogen is lighter than oxygen, and had gravitation decided the position of the latter, it would have formed a stratum of irrespirable and inflammable gas about two miles in depth over the carbon.

The theory, therefore, does not provide for such results, or such a state of things as actually exists in the atmosphere, or in any other department of physical nature. It does not provide for the due proportionate adjustment of the primordial elements, supposing them to have been created separately, nor for the continuance or permanence of any combination, whether in the atmosphere or the earth, when formed. It needs to a far greater extent than the Scripture doctrine of the creation of the heavens and earth in a perfect state, the constant agency of the Creator in respect to every department, every item, and every condition of his physical works. For in the one case the requisite proportions and combinations were established and perfected at the outset, while in the other they were left to occupy incalculable periods of duration. In order to the production of such results as exist in the composition of the atmosphere, the earth, and the organized forms of existence, there must be a perfect adaptation and adjustment to each other, of the requisite elements in respect to their *properties* and *quantities*, and in the relation of the bodies constituted, in respect to both *space* and *time*. And the perfections of the Creator, as exhibited in his works of creation, surely require us to regard those works in the perfect adjustments and combinations which pervade the realms of nature and give stability and beauty to the material and visible universe, and render it suitable to be the scene of his moral administration, and of the agency of his rational and accountable creatures.

This theory of primordial elements, and of the production from them, by the operation of their laws, "of all the forms and changes of organic and inorganic nature," past, present, and future, as promulgated in this age of chemical science, is puerile and contemptible, compared with the fortuitous combination of atoms or elements conceived of by a Grecian sage more than two thousand years ago; or with the quality of circular motion imagined by Des Cartes before the laws of chemistry were known to be inherent in the particles of matter, and productive of the phenomena of the physical world.

In presence of this theory of elements, what has heretofore been called natural theology, must resign its pretensions. For on this theory the argument of design must be restricted to what takes place in the laboratory of nature. If there was any design in creating elements with certain properties the operation of which we call laws, then, so far as any inferences from the results can be made on this theory, the design was limited to that operation. For the properties in question can operate only in certain fixed and unalterable modes, and can only produce certain fixed and uniform results; when they have combined and operated their work is done and their power exhausted. Certain physical changes have been produced, by certain physical causes; all which might just as well happen if nothing more was to follow, (and according to the theory in question, nothing more did follow for myriads of ages) as if an endless series of other things of other natures were to be produced by other causes. And if the causes of geological phenomena which science observes, exist in the elements of matter, and the results are ascribed to the operations of those causes, science will reject the supposition of any other cause, physical or Divine, as unnecessary and unphilosophical; and on that theory natural theology can make no inference in relation to a supreme, intelligent, first cause. It may be condescendingly admitted that the primordial elements may have been created by such a first cause; but the theory is quite as complete without, as with such admission. All that the theory requires is, the fact that such simple elements exist; that in certain conditions and relations they will operate; and that their operation, time enough being granted, will produce the physical phenomena which the geologist observes. Many, however, adopt this theory, who would be shocked at the idea of their being thought deficient of reverence for the Creator, or for the revelation He has made.

How different would be the conclusion, if arguing without any reference to what is revealed in the Scriptures, we first assumed that there is an infinite, self-existent Being, possessed of all possible perfections; that He is the Creator of this and of all worlds and creatures; that He exerted His creative power solely for moral reasons and purposes, and made the material world as a stage or scene for the manifestation of His perfections, the emanations of His goodness, the administration of His moral government, the exhibition of His works of providence and grace: And, that, being absolutely perfect, and acting according to His perfections, all His works, of whatever description, must necessarily be perfect in their kinds, and according to their several natures: Should we not, in that case, infer of course and without hesitation that since the globe as a scene of such administration, would be better fitted and more perfect by having its material elements united and combined in such manner and degree as to require no changes in order to its utmost perfection, than by having its elements in their crude separate state, so as to require an endless series of operations to combine and bring them into the destined condition of the fabric;—should we not unavoidably infer, that the earth as created was perfect, and had its elements in a perfect state of combination? Would not a contrary supposition grossly detract from our idea of the perfections and purposes of the Creator?

And if, on examining the earth, we found it on and beneath the surface, teeming with evidences of change, its materials confused and distorted like a mass of ruins, its interior a charnel house of relics of organic natures, should we not with equal confidence infer, that these phenomena had been caused subsequently to its creation and its primeval state of perfection?—And that they had been caused for reasons not founded in the nature or the original condition and purpose of the earth, but founded in some infraction or obstruction of that purpose? And if next, we examined the phenomena of man as a moral and accountable agent, his manifest declension from a perfect state, the corruption of his heart, the depravity of his will, his disordered affections, his evil passions, his evil conduct, his debasement, his boding fears, his misery, his pains, sicknesses, and death, should we not conclude, that on account of his defection and consequently of a necessary change of his destiny, the Creator had blighted the earth, filled it with relics and monuments of his displeasure, and rendered it suitable to be the habitation of man in his fallen state?

Suppose now a Pythagoras or a Socrates to have groped his way thus far, by the lights of nature, and then to have been furnished with the Scriptures of the Old Testament, and to have received them with confidence and faith; would he not behold there a plain, consistent, and ample account of the whole matter, confirmatory and essentially conformable to his previous conclusions? Would not his reverence of the all-perfect Creator, withhold him from imputing to that Being the creation of imperfect, incomplete, incongruous works, which time and change had not remedied, and which no conceivable amount of physical changes could ever render perfect. Would he not say, I might as well ascribe perfection to a builder who without even deciding the plan, dimensions, or object of his mansion, should merely plant the seeds of trees, which, in course of time, might furnish timber for its frame work ; or to a treatise of philosophy towards the writing of which the author had proceeded no further than to select the forms of the letters of the language to be instituted and employed by him in his composition ? or to a machine, the inventor of which had only selected the materials to be employed in its construction ? And would he not recoil from saying with Doctor Buckland, in his Bridgewater Treatise : "If geology should seem to require some little *concession* from the literal interpreter of Scripture, it may fairly be held to *afford ample compensation* for this demand, by the large additions it has made to *the evidences of natural religion ?*"

What should we think of a philosopher, who, in order to obtain a clearer, more simple, and more profound impression, of the grandeur and poetic beauty of Milton's "Paradise Lost," than could be derived from it in its existing form as a literary composition, —should before perusing it, request the printer to furnish him with the physical elements, the metallic letters, the vowels, the consonants, the diphthongs, the marks of interpunction, and all the other visible constituents combined in the words and sentences of the poem, that he might judge of the work, by studying its primordial elements; and from the mode in which he found them capable of being combined by an euphonical collocation of the types, should infer a *theory of the mode* in which the sightless poet had constructed his wonderful Epic: And having thus obtained what appeared to him to be a glimpse of the genius of poetry, should regard his theory of elementary, typographical composition, as the only thing of importance to be contended for in relation to the origin, perfection, meaning, purpose, or end, of a poem? Should we not conclude, that he was addled and infatuated by his hypothesis to such a degree, that if Milton were alive and should make oath that he neither proceeded upon the alleged theory, nor could in any way admit or sanction it, he would, in the sullenness of pride and vanity, refuse to believe him!

CHAPTER IX.

No theory of the mode of Causation necessary to the credit of Revelation, or to our faith in it.—The possibility of the former Continents with their Animal and Vegetable races, having been merged and suspended in the waters of the Deluge, and transferred to the bed of the former seas, and there deposited in the existing strata, considered.

Neither the credit of Revelation itself, nor the faith of those who believe in it, demands any such theory as the geologists furnish, or any other theory, or attempt to explain the *mode* of producing the changes which the phenomena of the earth exhibit. And if the Scriptures do not inform us of moral reasons for those changes we must be content to be ignorant as to why, or how, they were produced. It is not in man, nor in science at any stage of its advancement, to explain how they were operated, or to assign for them reasons worthy of the Creator whom the Scriptures reveal.

But if any explanation derived from the Scriptures

themselves were called for, a far more credible and satisfactory one than that of the geologists, might easily be furnished. The only catastrophe affecting the condition of the whole earth, of which the Scriptures inform us, was the Noachic Deluge. For that visitation, however great its extent and its effects, adequate moral reasons are assigned.

Now let it be considered that we are wholly ignorant as to what was the condition of the materials of the crust of the globe originally, and at that epoch. For aught that we know, they may have been free from rock of any description, to the depth of ten miles or more; the same materials which are now separated into different mineral beds and layers may have been mixed in such proportions as at once to have constituted the most prolific soil for the growth of vegetation and the support of animals; and to be dissolved, held suspended in the waters of the deluge, and by chemical processes, separated, precipitated, and petrified in the mineral masses which now exist. As now separated, no one of those masses is, without mixture with others, adapted to animal or vegetable life. In proportion as they are duly mixed, they become productive. And for aught that we know, they may, when perfectly mixed, originally, and during the ages preceding the deluge, have sustained such variety and abundance of vegetable and animal races, as at the epoch of that visitation, to supply all the fossil remains which geology discovers or implies.

This theory, if it be one, accounts for the quantity and the universal presence of water, necessary in the formation of each and every one of the sedimentary deposits; for the distribution and intermixture of both marine and terrestrial plants and animals in the successive beds or strata; for the marked difference in the mineral composition of the different beds, which no other theory pretends in any degree to account for; and finally for the otherwise reasonless and unaccountable changes in the geological condition of the earth of which there is such abundant and resistless evidence.

And admitting all that the geologists tell us of the most imperfect of the organic races being lowest down in the fossiliferous beds; what can be more obvious than to suppose that as the waters of the deluge rose, and progressively became charged with sedimentary matter, shell-fish should have been stifled and buried, before the placoids, ganoids, or other species of fish, fishes before reptiles, reptiles before birds, and birds before quadrupeds? On this theory such order of deposition would be as natural and obvious, as it is necessary to the latest geologic hypothesis. And if there are particular facts which this theory will not explain, they are facts which are explainable upon no theory yet promulgated.

The principal geological writers exhibit to us tabular charts, classifying and noting the distribution of the fossil relics of plants and animals as hitherto discovered in the successive sedimentary formations from the lowest to the highest. Taking that of Professor Hitchcock as an example, we find in the lowest fossiliferous group, comprising the cambrian and the silurian rocks, marine shells, molluscous, radiated, and articulated animals, and fishes ; and various plants both terrestrial and marine.

In the next, the carboniferous group, the same variety of plants, with the addition of pines, palms, and others ; and of animals, with the addition of fresh-water shells, insects, reptiles, and some species of fishes.

In the next, the red sandstone group, while the variety prevailing lower down seems diminished, there is an addition to the preceding lists of birds, tortoises, several of the largest species of reptiles, and of fishes, and some species of plants.

In the succeeding groups, the oolite, the cretaceous, and the tertiary, very numerous marine and terrestrial plants and animals are found ; the land animals prevailing chiefly in the tertiary formation, towards the superior portion of which the deer, the horse, the ox, the elephant, mastodon, and other of the largest species of quadrupeds occur ; of marine animals, the dolphin, seal, walrus, and others; and of birds the pelican, buzzard, lark, duck, and others.

Such lists or classifications are doubtless imperfect, and may be subject to revision and improvement by further discoveries. Still from the occurrence and seeming prevalence for the most part of the least perfect classes of animals in the lowest fossiliferous formations, the more perfect higher up, and the most perfect, especially of land animals in the highest portions, the geologists deduce very important inferences: Such as, that prior to the first inhumation of animal remains, the planet was in so imperfect a condition as to preclude the existence of animal life; that when by geological changes, the washing down of rocks, and diffusion of sediment, it was so far improved as to admit of organized existences, those animals were created whose relics were first inhumed; that these, and all their successors, were buried by the gradual deposit of sedimentary matter; that from period to period as the earth was improved in its condition, new and superior races of plants and animals were created, and each in turn deposited and fossilized.

These inferences depend wholly and absolutely upon the assumption that the sedimentary beds were formed by the almost imperceptibly slow aggregation of matter derived from primitive rocks, and consequently that the fossils which are lowest down in the stratified rocks are the remains of plants and animals, which lived at the remote period when the sedimentary process had reached no greater height. If the sedimentary beds were not formed in the manner which their theory assumes, then the inference of successive creations of new and more perfect races at widely separated intervals has no foundation. The character and relative position of the fossil relics in the rocks, does not prove that the rocks themselves were formed by the supposed inconceivably slow process. It is indeed far more conceivable and credible that the same relics should be fixed in the same positions by a rapid than by a slow process.

Let the circumstances and requisite conditions in the two cases be considered.

In the one case, when, according to the geologic theory, the deposit of sediment began, the solid surface both beneath the ocean and above the sea level was granite. There was no soil for the support of plants or animals; and if there were any plants, insects, shell-fish, or other organized existences in the fresh or salt-waters, none of them are supposed to have been fossilized during the vast period occupied in the formation of the group of rocks termed non-fossiliferous, which rests on the granite, since there no such relics have been discovered. When that group was completed, and the next, the Cambrian, had commenced, various marine shells, radiated and articulated animals, fishes, marine plants and land plants, were supplied for inhumation.

It is apparent from this list *of marine* fossils, as from other considerations, that the scene of their deposit was beneath the waters of the ocean ; and from the reported thickness of the superimposed masses, this must have been at a depth of some six or seven miles below the surface of the sea. Of course, no plants or animals of any description could possibly subsist at that depth, nor probably at one-twentieth part of such a distance below the surface. Nor could they, without a miracle, be precipitated from near the surface to such a depth, or anything more than a fractional part of it. Dead fishes, radiated and articulated animals, and plants, it is presumed would not sink at all. Nor indeed is it conceivable that the finely comminuted sedimentary matter of the successive groups of rocks, supposing it to have been slowly disengaged from the original granite, and diffused in the waters of the ocean, should ever slowly subside and sink down miles below the surface. And surely nothing can be more incredible, than that land plants, after being drifted into and widely dispersed near the surface of the ocean, should be precipitated to the depth of five or six miles, and there in the course of time be buried up and fossilized in a perfect state of preservation, notwithstanding the lapse of time between their detachment from the soil, and their inhumation, and the action on them of river and ocean currents, and of salt, carbonic acid, and other corroding agents in the sea.

It is clear that the first sedimentary deposits must have been made at the supposed depth of eight or ten miles below the sea level; for otherwise they could not have risen to the height of eight or ten miles above the subjacent granite. To suppose that when they commenced, the granite platform beneath them was within a moderate distance of the surface, and was from time to time forced down by some convulsion, may seem to remove one difficulty, but only by creating another. For on that supposition, where were the waters of the ocean, which though they now occupy about three-fourths of the surface of the globe, are from two or three to nine or more miles in depth? From the universality of the gneiss, the lowest of the sedimentary rocks; the regular succession of the beds and groups above it, and the necessary constancy of the action of the natural causes by which the granite rocks are supposed to have been worn down, it follows that the process of sedimentary formations must have been universally constant over the whole area occupied by them, and therefore if the waters of the ocean had been shallow enough to admit of the deposition of sediment, and of plants and animals, there would not have been room enough for them, even had they overspread the entire surface of the globe.

All the geologists agree that the stratified rocks were deposited from water, and therefore originally must have been nearly horizontal. The total thickness of the fossiliferous strata generally is held to be about seven miles, and that of the non-fossiliferous supposed to be three miles or more. Organic remains, relics of plants and animals, occur more or less in all the fossiliferous strata. "It is," says Professor Hitchcock, "a moderate estimate to say, that two-thirds of our existing continents are composed of fossiliferous rocks. This estimate," he adds, "might without exaggeration be confined to strata that contain *marine* relics which were deposited beneath the ocean."

The fossiliferous strata, therefore (and consequently the non-fossiliferous beneath them), must, as has been before observed, have been elevated from beneath the ocean, after the whole process of stratification was completed; for otherwise the upper stratum of the series with its imbedded fossils could not have been formed. The whole mass must have remained beneath the ocean, and substantially in the position in which the sediment was deposited, till the operation was finished. It could not, maintaining its horizontal position, have been gradually elevated, and yet have left room for the ocean water without deluging the dry land and precluding the existence of land plants, and animals, to be inhumed in the uppermost fossiliferous stratum, where they chiefly occur; nor could it at any stage before its completion, have been tilted up and distorted as it now is, without precluding the orderly horizontal deposition of the strata still to be formed.

From these and other considerations, not necessary now to be insisted on, we are entitled to infer that the elevation of our present continents and their mountain ranges was subsequent to the deposition of the fossiliferous strata, and was sudden, and occupied but a brief space of time. That it was violent, is shown by the tilted and distorted positions which in many localities the whole mass of sedimentary matter, from the lowest stratum to the highest, now exhibits; and also from the height to which the mountains, capped with sedimentary rocks, were raised; it being known that in the Alps such rocks abound with organic remains from six to eight thousand feet above the level of the sea; in the Pyrenees, nearly as high; in the Andes at the height of fourteen thousand feet, and on the Himalaya summits at a still greater altitude. That the elevating force must have been simultaneously exerted in all the regions occupied by the present continents, is to be inferred from the unquestionable necessity there was of removing and sinking the former continents, and thereby filling the vacuum caused by elevating new ones, and at the same time providing a capacious bed for the present ocean.

That the elevatory force by which the present continents were raised, was exerted after and within a limited period after the completion of the sedimentary strata, is further evident from the fact that the dykes and veins of mineral and metallic matter which rise from beneath to the surface, were not forced up till after those strata were raised, tilted, and fixed in their present position ; as appears from the fact that those dykes and veins in passing through inclined and distorted strata, pierce them not at right angles with their planes, but obliquely, and maintain in general a vertical direction which could not have happened till after the stratified masses had been forced up.

The reader will now consider the facts thus briefly glanced at : That all the sedimentary rocks which constitute the field of geologic research and hypothesis, were formed beneath the waters of the ocean ; that the fossiliferous groups, to the depth of about seven miles, contain both marine and terrestrial plants and animals : That these and the sedimentary group beneath them were deposited prior to their elevation above the sea level ; that the continents previously occupied by vegetable and animal races were removed or depressed at the same time or immediately after the present continents were raised ; and in view of these facts, and the inferences which they justify, he will be prepared to decide whether it is possible that the stratified rocks were formed, and their fossils distributed and buried up in them, in the manner represented by the geological theory ; or whether a process like that above indicated, by which the whole mass of. sedimentary matter was dissolved, intermixed with the existing plants and animals, and held in solution in the waters of the deluge ; and under the influence of mechanical, chemical, galvanic, electric, and perhaps other forces, precipitated, distributed into beds of diverse mineral composition, consolidated, and subsequently elevated above the sea level.

In noting the difficulties of the former supposition, it must be observed, that the present continents occupy the space, which prior to the sedimentary formations, was occupied by the ocean ; and the present ocean occupies the field of the former continents. From those former continents therefore, the mass of sedimentary matter must have been derived, and likewise the terrestrial plants and animals which are fossilized. And it is further to be observed that both the marine and terrestrial plants and animals which are imbedded in the sedimentary rocks, are in general very perfectly preserved; a large portion of them in the limestones and other solid strata, exhibiting no marks of abrasion or decay

If then those former continents consisted of earths and soils adapted to the spontaneous and most exuberant growth of plants, and the support of every species of animals; and in that state were saturated, and with their various vegetable and animal races, diffused in the waters of the deluge, and in that state of mixture transferred to the area of the former seas; the conditions requisite to the sedimentary and fossil formations would be provided for; the pervading presence of water the medium of deposition; the distribution of diverse mineral matter into distinct beds; the mixture of marine and terrestrial plants and animals in the lower as well as the higher groups; and in latitudes and climates to which they were not indigenous; the aggregation of vegetable masses in the coal measures; the subsequent upheaval of the strata thus formed, to constitute the present continents, and the still later intrusion of mineral and metallic dykes and veins; and the formation of a bed for the present oceans.

Doubtless such a process was possible, and possible without any greater miracle than that of a universal deluge; possible, consistently with the wide dispersion of the fossil relics, and the state of preservation in which they are discovered; possible, with the materials thus indicated, and consistently with the separation of them into strata of different mineral composition; possible, consistently with the moral reasons assigned in Scripture for the deluge itself, and the results consequent upon it, in shortening the period of human life; the necessity of toil and of arts and inventions to render the earth productive; the allowance of animal food for the sustenance of man; the extinction of many species of plants and animals, consequent on the sterility of the new formations; the spontaneous growth of noxious in place of healthful plants; the introduction of diseases, droughts, famines, pestilences, poverty, and oppression; and lastly, possible, consistently with what is prophetically foreshown of the purpose of the Creator, hereafter, not by a protracted, but by a summary process, to renovate, remodel, and re-establish the earth in its primitive paradisiacal condition of fertility, healthfulness, and beauty. And if with these conditions such a process was possible, the purpose of these observations requires no more.

That a transfer of the superior portion of the former continents, with their animal tribes, to the scene of the sedimentary formations, should not have involved a coincident transfer of the human with the inferior races, and a mixture of their relics with the flora and fauna of the rocks, may have a reason in what relates to the resurrection, and the relation of its period to that of the future renovation of the earth; or if they were transferred, further investigations may yet disclose them ; or their place of sepulture may be beyond the limits of geologic exploration and research.

Supposing the deluge to have been instrumental in producing the great geologic changes referred to, their congruity with the teachings of inspiration is, in the most important particulars, sufficiently apparent. The earth, its vegetation, the inferior tribes of animals, and man, were created perfect in their natures, and in relation to their respective objects and destinations. The earth was perfectly fitted to be the perpetual abode of man in his primeval state of holiness and happiness. Man was invested with dominion over all inferior creatures. The rites and services necessary to his social and religious well-being were instituted. Vegetables were appointed for his sustenance. Man apostatised, renounced his allegiance to the Creator, forfeited the gifts and immunities of his previous state, was judged and condemned. A change in his physical condition and destiny was denounced upon him, corresponding to the change in his moral character, relations, and prospects. The physical was the consequence, the legitimate and appropriate consequence, of the moral change. His apostacy, considered in itself, and as involving his own race in its moral, and his own with the inferior races, in its physical consequences, was an event of incomparably more importance than any other event which ever affected this world. The earth, polluted by his sin, was doomed and smitten. The Creator said to Adam, "Cursed is the ground for thy sake; in sorrow shalt thou eat of it all the days of thy life; thorns also and thistles shall it bring forth to thee, and thou shalt eat the herb of the field; in the sweat of thy face shalt thou eat bread, till thou return into the ground; for out of it wast thou taken; for dust thou art, and unto dust shall thou return." Man was no longer permitted to subsist on the fruits of paradise. He was driven forth from Eden, to till the ground from which he was taken.

Under this sentence for about sixteen centuries, the period of human life was prolonged to eight or nine hundred years; the sentence being but partially executed. The respite was abused. "All flesh corrupted his way. The wickedness of man was great in the earth; every imagination of the thoughts of his heart was only evil continually. The earth was corrupt. And the Lord said, I will destroy man whom I have created, from the face of the earth, both man and beast, and the creeping thing, and the fowls of the air—the end of all flesh is come before me; for the earth is filled with violence through them; and behold *I will destroy them with the earth—I, even I, do bring a flood of waters upon the earth, to destroy all flesh wherein is the breath of life, from under Heaven: and every thing that is in the earth shall die.*—And every living substance was destroyed which was upon the face of the ground, both man and cattle, and the creeping things, and the fowl of the heavens; and they were destroyed from the earth; and Noah only remained alive, and they that were with him in the ark."

This deluge continued during twelve months and ten days; a period far longer than was necessary to the destruction of animal and vegetable life, and long enough it may be assumed, considering the object of it, and the agencies employed in effecting it, to produce all the geological changes which can be ascribed to it. It is noticeable that, vegetation having been destroyed, Noah continued in the ark nearly two months after the face of the ground was dry; within which time, a supply of vegetation for the animals in the ark, might be produced.

The greatness of the catastrophe, considered in its physical as well as its moral relations, is indicated by what took place after its termination. The Lord said —"I will not again *curse* the ground any more for man's sake—neither will I again *smite* any more every thing living, as I have done. While the earth remaineth, seed time and harvest, and cold and heat, and summer and winter, and day and night, shall not cease." For man's security and sustentation, under his altered and novel circumstances, the fear of him was impressed on all the inferior creatures, and the flesh of animals was allowed to him for food. His offering of sacrifices was accepted, and some important moral precepts were enjoined upon him. And further to confirm his confidence in the future exemption of the earth from a similar visitation, and to commemorate the wonders of the recent scene, a covenant between the Creator and his creatures, was announced, and a token of it, visible to all creatures, was established. "And God spake unto Noah and to his sons with him, saying: and I, behold, I establish my covenant with you, and with your seed after you, and with every living creature that is with you, of the fowl, of the cattle, and of every beast of the earth with you, from all that go out of the ark, to every beast of the earth. And God said, This is the token of the covenant which I make, between Me and you and every living creature that is with you, for perpetual generations. I do set my bow in the cloud, and it shall be for a token of a covenant between Me and the earth. And it shall come to pass, when I bring a cloud over the earth, that the bow shall be seen in the cloud: And I will remember My covenant which is between Me and you and every living creature of all flesh; and *the waters shall no more become a flood to destroy all flesh.* And the bow shall be in the cloud; and I will look upon it, that I may remember the everlasting covenant between God and every living creature of all flesh, that is upon the earth. And God said unto Noah, This is the token of the covenant which I have established between Me and all flesh that is upon the earth."

The apostacy of man was, in its nature as a moral phenomenon, and in its moral and physical consequences and relations, the most comprehensive and disastrous event, of which the earth has ever been the scene. It involved the character and destiny of the whole race. As an example of revolt, renunciation of allegiance, alienation and antagonism, against the Creator and moral ruler of the universe, it bore direct and manifest relations to the unfallen myriads of other worlds. It was the rebellion of a province of the moral empire. It was the act of a bodied race of creatures, visible by their physical organizations; and was visibly manifested by their external agency. Its nature, turpitude, and deserts, were therefore to be signified by external, physical, and visible inflictions; decay and death to man's physical nature, as a concomitant and counterpart to the spiritual death and doom of his immortal soul; and a visible confirmatory, and illustrative, physical change, in his terrestrial habitation and condition. Hence the specification of physical evils in the sentence pronounced upon Adam, and the order in which they are recorded. *Cursed* is the earth

—for thy sake—henceforth in sorrow shalt thou partake of its products. Thorns and thistles shall it bring forth to thee. In the sweat of thy face shalt thou eat bread till thou return to the dust. These terms denote vast and various physical changes ; changes suitable to indicate the total change in man's moral character, relations, and destiny; changes proportioned in other respects to that stamped on his mortal prospects by the introduction of toil, sorrow, decay, and death. But the perfect rectitude of the Lawgiver and judge in these inflictions would not, we may suppose, have been so convincingly manifest to Adam and his successors, as to induce their full recognition and acknowledgment, had they been executed immediately, or before the desperate alienation, corruption, and wickedness of men, in their fallen state, had been manifested by a prolonged trial, attended by every advantage of outward and temporal circumstances : A respite was therefore permitted. The days of Adam and those of his immediate descendants were protracted to about nine hundred years ; the earth probably continuing to yield spontaneously its primeval fruits, till the lapse of 1600 years ; when the world was so filled with corruption and violence as to forbid further delay, require an immediate and summary execution of the curse upon the earth, in connection with all but a total extinction of the race, and such changes in the surface, the climates, and the products of the globe, and such abridgement, toil, and sorrow of post-diluvian life as visibly and fully to comport with the terms of the primeval sentence, and to vindicate the righteousness and the necessity of it, to the view of the whole universe; and moreover to leave in the condition of its rocks and relics such tokens of the nature, occasion, and effects of the visitation, as should never be called in question, at least by any other than fallen creatures.

This, like other extraordinary dispensations affecting the whole race, or particular nations, or communities, was expressly declared to be the effect of immediate Divine interposition. It was a judicial visitation on the race for their apostacy and wickedness. "Behold I, even I, do bring a flood of waters upon the earth, to destroy all flesh," &c. It was signalized by numerous outward and visible arrangements and instrumentalities, betokening the nature and greatness of the exigency, and adapted to convince all created intelligences of the presence and righteousness of its author. That there was great significance in the visibility, as well as in the magnitude of the physical changes, considered as the tokens or counterpart of the moral changes wrought by the apostacy, and rendered manifest by the universal corruption and violence which ensued; can admit of no rational doubt, whether considered with relation to intelligent spectators of the scene, fallen and unfallen, or with relation to all subsequent observation of the physical effects and monuments of those changes.

The scene which from the beginning has been passing upon this earth, is doubtless a spectacle to the universe of created intelligences. From the beginning the rights and prerogatives of the Creator, as moral and providential ruler, have been questioned, denied, and arrogantly usurped by the fallen. Instead of rendering to Him the homage and obedience which He claims, they yield themselves to the rival system of idolatry, and visibly manifest the depravity of their hearts, by worshipping and serving creatures. On numerous occasions therefore, when their corruptions could no longer be permitted, he has come forth, and by local and visible interpositions and enduring effects and monuments of his righteous indignation has rebuked and confounded their impiety. Sometimes, as on occasion of the confusion of tongues and dispersion of mankind to all parts of the earth, and on that of the destruction of Sodom, and that of the destruction of the nations of Canaan, He "who was in the beginning and by whom all things in heaven and earth, were created," signalized his interposition by his visible presence, as if, in view of an observant universe, to attest and sanction by his personal appearance and inspection, the necessity and propriety of the visitations about to be effected by His power. Has it, since the audacious and idolatrous project of Nimrod and his confederates was defeated, been possible for any intelligent observer of the actual condition of the nations and tribes of mankind with their thousand variant and discordant languages, to doubt of the greatness and universality of the interposition which "scattered them abroad upon the face of all the earth," and confounded "the language of all the earth?" Or could such an observer possibly doubt of the reality, the far-reaching import, the sufficiency and moral necessity of the reason assigned for the visitation which has left its impress as it were upon the very nature and the social condition of every nation, tribe, family, and individual of the race down to the present hour? Would there have been anything extravagant in arguing from the local phenomena of the Dead Sea and the historical facts of its history, that it was, for the reason assigned, miraculously constituted, a perpetual memorial and witness of the righteous judgement of God; or the adequacy of the reason assigned for so total and remediless a destruction; even if the apostle Peter had not compared it to the dejection and doom of the angels who fell, and with the destruction of the earth by "bringing in the flood upon the world of the ungodly:" and then describing it as "a turning of the cities of Sodom and Gomorrah into ashes, condemning them with an overthrow and making them an example," a monitor, a warning, "unto those that should after live ungodly?" "Set forth," saith St. Jude, "for an example, suffering the vengeance of eternal fire."

Now if the nature and extent of the outward and visible results in these cases were only proportioned to the wickedness exhibited in these local and limited scenes of action, why should we hesitate to infer the vastness and universality of the physical changes at the deluge, when for their original apostacy and their universal wickedness, the whole race excepting Noah and his family were with the inferior animals to be whelmed in utter and indiscriminate destruction?

In the Psalms, and other parts of Scripture this visitation is alluded to as among the most wondrous interpositions of the Ruler of the Universe. The covenant with Noah was of such significance as to be referred to by Isaiah in confirmation of the sacredness and stability of the eternal covenant between God and his redeemed people. "As I have sworn that the waters of Noah should no more go over the earth, so have I sworn that I would not be wroth with thee nor rebuke thee. For the mountains shall depart and the hills be removed; but my kindness shall not depart from thee, neither shall the covenant of my peace be removed, saith the Lord that hath mercy on thee."—*Isaiah* 54. The Apostle Peter contrasts the destruction of the earth by the deluge, with its future transformation by fire, indicating the universality of the physical results. "The world that then was, being overflowed with water, perished. But the heavens and earth which are now, by the same word are kept in store, reserved unto fire against the day of judgment and perdition of ungodly men."

CONCLUSION.

Reference to the Supreme authority and importance of the Scriptures.

If the Scriptures were given by inspiration of the Creator and Ruler of the World; if they teach what we are to believe concerning Him, and what duties He requires of us; if they record His acts as Creator and Ruler, and the laws and sanctions of His moral government; then they demand our highest reverence as bearing the signatures and sanctions of His infinite authority, exhibiting the nature and basis of His prerogatives and rights, and imposing upon us the most unrestricted and imperative obligations. If in our degeneracy and blindness we do not understand and comprehend all that they teach, it becomes us to regard them as the appointed vehicle, the ark, of the Divine wisdom, authority and favor to a fallen race, and at least to refrain from putting forth the presumptuous hand of our physical theories to rectify or guide it.

Infidelity, driven forth from the fields of metaphysics and philosophy, has taken refuge in the dark recesses and labyrinths of physical nature, where its invariable concomitant and counterpart, superstition, finds mysteries, prodigies, paradoxes, and wonders, suited to its insatiable cravings. The christian man is tempted to follow, and to encounter the wily enemy in this ambush, leaving neglected behind him the only citadel and tower of his strength and safety, with its munitions of defence. He ventures on the conflict with such weapons only as he may have in common with, or may obtain from the adverse party, by barter or concession. If, on this arena, he contends for the reality and divine authority of inspiration or of miracles, he soon, step by step, as the spell of naturalism, and of his contrasted and conscious weakness comes over him, yields to the visible, innumerable, inexplicable paradoxes, mysteries, and mazes of nature, all that his adopted guides, the laws of physical science, reject as supernatural. As he descends into the sepulchral abysses of the earth in search of primeval records and revelations, the light of heaven is intercepted and soon forgotten. (*See Appendix C.*)

If in respect to the moral nature, accountability, and destiny of man, in his relations to his Creator,

Preserver, Ruler, and Redeemer, the Bible is anything, it is without competition or comparison, essential to him; his only infallible guide, a lamp to his feet, a light to his path. Suited to his limited capacities, his dependence and his weakness, it exhibits moral reasons for the works of creation and providence, and leaves the great, and to him inscrutable mysteries of nature, and of the mode of the Creator's agency in originating, upholding, changing, and governing, all things, unexplained.

Jehovah, the Incarnate Word, is, in the theories of physical science, unrecognized and unacknowledged. When He was visibly in the world which was made by Him, the world knew him not. And that He is now no more known or acknowledged in the systems of Idealism, Pantheism, and Naturalism, than in those of Pagan superstition and Mahommedan imposture, should be a warning to good men not to swerve from the lights of the only revelation He has vouchsafed and sanctioned for their guidance. As yet the world at large has never acknowledged His prerogatives and rights as Creator and Moral Governor. But we are forewarned in terms fitted to arrest and fix our attention, that in the consummation of the purposes, and as one of the results of his perfect administration, He will be recognized in the greatness and majesty of His person, and the glory of His attributes; every eye shall see Him, and every knee shall bow, and every tongue confess that, in contradistinction to all idols and all creatures, He is Jehovah, the self-existent, the creator, upholder, ruler, and judge of all.

APPENDIX.

A.

[From a vol. entitled "Geological Cosmogony," published by ROBERT CARTER, 1843.]

"THE following extracts from different works on Geology will sufficiently indicate the views of the authors on the points to which they relate.

"As the materials of stratified rocks are in great degree derived directly or indirectly from those which are unstratified, we commence our inquiry at that most ancient period when there is much evidence to render it probable that the entire materials of the globe were in a fluid state, and that the cause of this fluidity was heat. The form of the earth being that of an oblate spheriod—is that which a fluid mass would assume from revolution around its axis. The nebular hypothesis offers the most simple and therefore the most probable theory respecting the first condition of the material elements that compose our solar system."—*Buckland.*

"The nebular hypothesis in its relations to the planetary system may be termed complete; it comprehends its beginnings, establishes those elements on which its duration depends, and exhibits the causes and mode of its ultimate transition into a novel form; and thus surveying it from its commencement to its close, we are as if in possession of that primeval Creative Thought which originated our system, and planned and circumscribed its destiny." "If that nebular hypothesis be true, all the forces developed upon the surface of our planet, and which have given rise to geological transitions, stretching through periods in which the existence of the human race is an invisible spec, will have resulted during a stage of condensation in a secondary nebula, which no instrument from any fixed star could possibly detect." "Our supposed origin of the planets gave them and their satellites that kind of orbits, and that kind of rotation, which produced their permanence; and the inherence of this same nebulous parentage, viz: the existence of an ether, leads gently to their decline."—*Nichol*, pp. 82, 106, 108.

"The nebular hypothesis, ridiculed as it has been by persons whose ignorance cannot excuse their presumption, is regarded as in a very high degree probable by some of the finest and most Christian minds. If I may venture to utter my own impressions, I must profess it as the most reasonable supposition, and the correllate of the nebular theory, that God originally gave being to the primordial elements of things, the very small number of simple bodies, endowing each with its own wondrous properties."—*Smith.*

"The evidence of geological phenomena constrains us to the belief, that our earth has existed, has been the seat of life, and has undergone many changes of its surface, through periods of time utterly beyond human power to assign. That evidence is of distinct and independent kinds, *chiefly* derived from the appearance of stratification and the remains of animal and vegetable life."—*Smith.*

"The best writers abound in general expressions; such as 'immense periods of time—undefined, yet countless ages—a duration to which we dare not assign a boundary—a work infinitely slow—a space of time from the contemplation of which the mind shrinks—a long succession of monuments, each of which may have required a thousand ages for its elaboration—successions of events where the language of nature signifies millions of years.'"—*Mantell, McCulloch, Sedgwick, and others, quoted by Smith.*

"The whole series of strata, from the earliest of them to the present surface of the globe, exhibits a body of evidence in favor of our doctrine [of antiquity]. Every stratum, partially excepting the limestones, consists of a mass of earthy matters which once formed the substance of rocks on elevated land. Those portions of the rocks have been separated from their parent masses, worn down, comminuted, transported often to great distances by the force of water, deposited, consolidated and hardened."—*Ibid.*

"Beneath the whole series of stratified rocks that appear on the surface of the globe, there probably exists a foundation of unstratified rocks, bearing an irregular surface, from the detritus of which the materials of stratified rocks have in great measure been derived either directly by the accumulation of the ingredients of disintegrated granite rocks ; or indirectly, by the repeated destruction of different classes of stratified rocks, the materials of which had, by prior operations, been derived from unstratified formations."—*Buckland.*

"In mountainous countries many facts are presented to the eye which approach to a standard of measurement of the average action of the atmosphere and of running water, in decomposing and washing off the surface of granitic and basaltic rocks. That action is sure and constant; but it is slow, to such a degree that not years, but centuries are required for its chronicle. Even the abrading of that description of rocks where they form the boldest sea-coast, by the violence of storms added to the ordinary action of water and weather (an addition of great power), has not materially altered the outline of such shores in Cornwall, the west and north of Scotland, Norway, and many other countries, since the beginning of our historical knowledge. But the action of a fresh water river infringing upon hard rocks, is much more feeble."—*Smith.*

"Every step we take in it [geology] forces us to make unlimited drafts on antiquity."—*Scrope, in Smith.*

"The detritus of the first dry lands, being drifted into the sea, and there spread out into extensive beds of mud, and sand, and gravel, would for ever have remained beneath the surface of the water, had not other forces been subsequently employed to raise them into dry land. These forces appear to have been the same expansive powers of heat and vapor, which, having caused the elevation of the first raised portions of the fundamental crystalline rocks, continued their energies through all succeeding geological epochs, and still exert them in producing the phenomena of active volcanoes."—*Buckland.*

"All observers admit that the strata were formed beneath the water, and have subsequently been converted into dry land."—*Ibid.*

"The first appearance of stratification is in the

rock called Gneiss. That is composed of the same materials as granite, on the irregular outline of which it rests. Over the Gneiss, come the beds of Mica, Schist, and Slates, whose thickness, 'like that of the Gneiss, cannot be ascertained, on account of the intervention of other rocks.' Their mode of formation is proved by the most striking characters to have been the same as that of the Gneiss. If we should venture to estimate the united thickness of this class, added to the Gneissic, at three or even four miles, we could not be charged with exaggeration."—*Smith.*

"The thickness of these strata we know to be enormous. These depths are discovered by geological observations and inferences—that they extend to many miles was also proved. We have every reason to know from what is taking place on our own earth, that the accumulation of materials at the bottom of the ocean, is a work *infinitely slow.* We are sure that such an accumulation as should produce the primary strata, as we now see them, must have occupied a space, from the contemplation of which the mind shrinks."—*McCulloch, as quoted by Smith.*

"Of the next group, the siliceous, slaty, and limestone aggregates, to which the name *Silurian system* is given,—the united thickness is about a mile and a half. Who then can calculate the periods of their derivation from the older formations, their deposition, their elevations, and distortions; their convulsions, penetrations, and alterations of the adjoining rocks, by *frequent* outbursts from the fiery liquid below, and other movements, till they were brought to their existing condition? It would seem perfectly impossible for any person, but moderately acquainted with the visible phenomena of volcanic regions, to escape the impression that myriads of ages must have been occupied in the production of these formations, before the creation of man and the adaptation of the earth's surface for his abode. Evidence to the same effect would accumulate upon us to a vast amount, in examining the old red sandstone, a remarkable deposit, several thousand feet in thickness, found in some parts of Great Britain, more abundantly in Ireland, and either in resemblance, or in equivalence, in many foreign regions. Next we come to the mountain limestone, consisting almost entirely of the shells and coralline productions of sea animals, often a thousand and more feet in thickness. This formation is frequently more or less interposed among the beds of coal, composed of compressed vegetable matter, underlaid and overlaid with shales, and sandstones in every variety; often effecting a thickness of three thousand feet. The new red sandstone advances us about another thousand feet.

"Other changes implying probably some alteration in the disposition, and consequently the action of the fiery gulf below, marked the next great system, or series of rocks,—the Oolitic. Its general thickness can be little less than half a mile. It is filled with the most convincing proofs of deposition from sea water both shallow and deep, the mingled waters of river mouths, and perhaps even fresh water of rivers and lakes.

"We arrive, in ascending, at the great masses of chalk, and its accompaniments of peculiar clays and sands, to the thickness of a thousand feet more. Though the lines of stratification are not here so visible as in the underlying formations, the evidence of deposition from watery mixture, and of very interesting effects from molecular and chemical attractions, is so clear as to be irresistible.

"Our last stage of ascent comprehends the tertiary series; a succession of beds, clays, sands, and limes, variously intermixed, occupying a thickness of six or eight hundred feet. When we have mounted to the most recent of those later formations, immediately below the soil on which we tread, we find enormous masses of gravel and other transported materials demonstrated by their position to have been rolled along by mighty currents, subsequently to all the lower formations.

"In those stratified rocks which are of a sandy constitution it is common to find pebbles, from the size of coriander seeds to that of birds' eggs, and much larger. These bear demonstrative evidence of having been derived from more ancient rocks, by fracture and detachment, *long rolling on a hard bottom under water*, dispersed through the loose sand of a deposit, *subsiding to the lower part* if a tolerably free motion were permitted, and then consolidated. Let the old red sandstone be our example. In many places the upper part of this vast formation is of a closer grain, showing that it was produced by the last and finest deposits of clayey and sandy mud, tinged as the whole is, with oxides and carbonates of iron, usually red but often of other hues. But frequently the lower portions, sometimes dispersed heaps, and sometimes the entire formation, consist of vast masses of conglomerate [pebbles with sand, &c].

"The earliest slate rocks, like all other strata, must have been originally deposited in a position horizontal or nearly so. By subsequent movements, not one but evidently many, they have been raised to all elevations, and bent to the utmost extent of contortion: as is shown by the lines of stratification.

"The stratification contains in itself the evidence of having required periods, impossible indeed to be determined by any assignment of figures, but to which, judging from all approximating evidence, our cycles of time afford none but a totally defective measure of comparison."—*Smith.*

"It appears that from the remotest periods there has been ever a coming in of new organic forms, and an extinction of those which pre-existed on the earth;

some species having endured for a longer, others for a shorter time; but none having reappeared after once dying out."—*Lyell*

"General and particular results all agree in demonstrating that the physical conditions of the ancient ocean must have been very different in some respects, from what obtain at present; and that these conditions were subject to great variation during the very long periods which elapsed in the formation of the crust of the earth. In the course of these changes, whole groups of animals perished; others were created to perish in their turn."—*Phillips.*

"The former universality of the ocean [is] now disproved by the discovery of the remains of terrestrial vegetation in strata of every age, even the most ancient."—*Lyell.*

"In an early part of our inquiry, we traced back the history of the primary rocks, which composed the first solid materials of the globe, to a probable condition of universal fusion, incompatible with the existence of any forms of organic life, and saw reason to conclude that as the crust of the globe became gradually reduced in temperature, the unstratified crystalline rocks, and stratified rocks produced by their destruction, were disposed and modified, during long periods of time, by physical forces, the same in kind with those which actually subsist, but more intense in their degree of operation; and that the result has been to adapt our planet to become the receptacle of divers races of vegetable and animal beings, and finally to render it a fit and convenient habitation for mankind." —*Buckland.*

"In the course of our inquiry, we have found abundant proofs, both of the beginning and the end of several successive systems of animal and vegetable life; each compelling us to refer its origin to the direct agency of creative interference."—*Ibid.*

"If geology should seem to require some little concession from the literal interpreter of Scripture, it may fairly be held to *afford ample compensation* for this demand, by the large additions it has made *to the evidences of natural religion*, in a department where revelation was not designed to give information."—*Ibid.*

"There are good grounds for supposing that, beyond a certain thickness for the solid crust of the earth, which can hardly be estimated at so much as *thirty* miles, the next contiguous matter is in a state of fusion, at a temperature probably higher than any that man can produce by artificial means; or any natural heat that can exist on the surface."

"All strata follow antecedent ones in an order which is certain and invariable for every region of the earth.

Nowhere, however, is the entire series found. Some member or many are wanting in every assignable locality; but they are never put in a violated order. The lower strata, manifestly the most early, are generally of the greatest extent in length and breadth, and very much the deepest in thickness. The higher and newer are severally of less magnitude in every dimension. Yet, in no case, must the idea of size or extent be taken upon a trifling scale. Even with the most recent, the area of one formation is often some hundreds of square miles."—*Smith.*

"There are thirty, or rather more, well defined *beds*, *layers*, or *strata*, of *different* mineral masses, (*different* in mineral composition,) lying upon each other, so as to form the surface of the globe on which we dwell. These combine themselves, by natural characters, into three or four grand groups. Compare them to a set of books, in thirty or forty volumes, piled up on their flat sides. They are placed one over the other, in a *sure* and *known* order of succession; that is, though in every locality some are wanting, the order of position is never violated."—*Ibid.*

"In the older fossiliferous rocks, animal life appears in as full a development with respect to *size*, as in the existing analogous animals. It does not appear that animal life, at that period, was limited with respect to number. The lower Silurian rocks are crowded, in some localities, with organic bodies; and their absence over extensive districts is only a condition in the distribution of testacea, &c., which prevails in our seas." —*Ibid.*

"In the superficial gravel containing rolled blocks of stone, coming from vast distances, we find bones of the elephant, rhinoceros, &c., of *extinct* species, mingled with bones of mammals of *known* species."—*Ibid.*

"The sources from which the matter of these ejected [volcanic] rocks ascend, are deeply seated beneath the granite; but it is not yet decided whether the immediate causes of an eruption be the access of water to local accumulations of the metalloid bases of the earths and alkalies; or whether lava be derived directly from that general mass of incandescent elements, which may probably exist at a depth of about one hundred miles beneath the surface of our planet. The intrusion both of dykes and irregular beds of unstratified crystalline matter, into rocks of every age and every formation, all proceeding upwards from an unknown depth, and often accumulated into vast masses, overlying the surface of stratified rocks, are phenomena co-extensive with the globe. Each individual movement [of the volcanic forces] has contributed its share towards the final object, of conducting the molten materials of an uninhabitable planet, through long successions of change and of convulsive movements, to a tranquil state of equilibrium ; in which it has become the convenient and delightful habitation of man, and of the multitudes of terrestrial creatures that are his fellow tenants of its actual surface."—*Buckland.*

"It is from the more ancient coal deposits that the most extraordinary evidence has been supplied in proof of the former existence of an extremely hot climate in those latitudes which are now the temperate and colder regions of the globe. It appears from the fossils of the carboniferous period, that the flora [contained] tree ferns, or plants allied to them, from forty to fifty feet in height; and arborescent lycopodiaceæ, from sixty to seventy feet high. Of the above classes of vegetables, the species are all small at present in cold climates;—their development even in the hottest parts of the globe, is now inferior to that indicated by the petrified forms of the coal formation. In regard to the geographical extent of the ancient vegetation, it was not confined, says M. Brongniart, to a small space, as to Europe for example; for the same forms are met with again at great distances. Thus the coal plants of North America are, for the most part, identical with those of Europe, and all belong to the same genera. The uninjured corals and chambered univalves of Melville Island [lat. 75°] and other high latitudes, sufficiently prove that, during the carboniferous period, there was an elevated temperature, even in northern regions bordering on the Arctic circle. The heat and humidity of the air, and the uniformity of climate, appear to have been most remarkable when the oldest strata hitherto discovered were formed. The approximation to a climate similar to that now enjoyed in these latitudes, does not commence till the era of the formations termed *tertiary;* and while the different tertiary rocks were deposited in succession, the temperature seems to have been still farther lowered, *and to have continued to diminish gradually, even after the appearance upon the earth of a great portion of the existing species.*"—*Lyell.*

"The upper bed of rock salt in Cheshire is twenty-six yards thick, and is separated from the lower bed of salt by a stratum of argillaceous stone ten yards thick. The lower salt has been penetrated forty yards. In another part of Cheshire three beds of rock salt have been found. The uppermost is four feet thick, the second twelve, and the lower has been penetrated twenty-five yards, but is not cut through. The rock salt at Cardona, in Spain, is 663 feet in height. Hungary and Poland afford the most numerous and extensive repositories of rock salt in Europe. The beds are inclined at an angle of 40°. There is an extensive formation stretching on each side of the Carpathian mountains for 600 miles. In the lofty deserts of Caramania in Asia,—in Great Tartary, Thibet, and Indostan, this mineral is also found. In the elevated mountains of

Peru, it is said to occur at the height of 9000 feet above the level of the sea. In the desert of Lybia there is an extensive bed; and it is found in South Africa, New South Wales, and in various islands."—*Bakewell.*

"Taken as an illustration of the structure of the crust of our globe, the successive coats of an onion, if they were of different colors, might not unaptly represent the different strata that cover certain districts. The different strata which occur under each other, are not arranged in the order of their density or specific gravity. Coal strata, for instance, are often covered with strata of iron stone, the specific gravity of which is more than twice that of coal. *Primitive rocks* were so called because no fossil remains of animals or vegetables, nor any fragments of other rocks, were found imbedded in them. Those rocks generally occur in immense masses or beds; they form the lowest part of the earth's surface with which we are acquainted, and constitute the foundation on which rocks of the other classes are laid. The rocks which immediately cover them contain, almost exclusively, the organic remains of the lowest class of animals. The lower series of *secondary rocks* are almost all distinctly stratified. Every regular stratum in which organic remains are disseminated, was once the uppermost rock, however deep it may be below the present surface. If it had been predicted a century ago, that a volume would be discovered, containing the natural history of the earliest inhabitants of the globe, which flourished and perished before the creation of man, what curiosity would have been excited to see this wonderful volume; how anxiously would philosophers have waited for the discovery! But this volume is now discovered; it is the volume of nature, rich with the spoils of primeval ages, unfolded to the view of the attentive observer, in the strata that compose the crust of the globe. Some of the more delicately constructed animals, and the fish whose bodies are found entire, imbedded in stone, appear to have been instantaneously destroyed and enveloped in mineral matter, before the putrefactive process could commence. Stratified rocks are composed of layers of stone, laid over each other, and divided by parallel seams like the leaves of a closed book. In these seams or partings, which divide the strata, there are frequently thin laminæ of soft earthy matter; but sometimes the surfaces of the upper and lower stratum are so closely joined that it requires a considerable force to separate them. The highest known point at which granite has been observed, in any part of the world, is Mont Blanc—15,680 feet above the level of the sea. In the northern or Swiss Alps, granite is seen only near their bases; the summits are composed of immense beds of stratified rocks. In the extensive range of the Andes, granite has not been found in a greater elevation than 11,500 feet. The summits of the Himmaleh mountains are believed to be composed of secondary strata. Though granite may be regarded as the lowest known rock formation, yet it is certain, that in many countries, the seat of volcanic fire is placed below granite. All rocks under the coal formation, belong either to the transition or primary class; and all the strata above the coal formation belong either to the upper, secondary, or the tertiary class. The different strata under a bed of coal are frequently similar to the strata over it; and the same series is again repeated under the lower beds of coal, and sometimes with a perfect similarity both in the succession and thickness of each. The thickness of the coal strata in the same coal-field often varies from a few inches to several yards; but each stratum generally preserves the same thickness throughout its whole extent. A dyke is a wall of mineral matter cutting through the strata in a position nearly vertical. The great coal formation appears to be confined to the lower secondary strata, generally resting on transition limestone. A remarkable coal formation occurs in Switzerland at the depth of 280 feet from the surface; over the coal there is a stratum of bituminous limestone, containing fluviatile shells, and bones and teeth of the large mammalia, particularly the teeth of a species of mastodon. Were it not for the organic remains in different rocks, we could not be certain that all rock formations were not contemporaneous. With respect to the identity of age, or what is pedantically named the synchronism of rock formations in distant countries, there can be little hesitation in admitting it, where the association with other rock formations is similar in both countries. The disintegration of rocks and mountains is constantly taking place by the incessant operation of the elements."—*Bakewell.*

"The following Geological doctrines are derived from the preceding extracts, and others elsewhere inserted, and from other passages in the writings of the same authors.

1. That the globe was at first in a state of igneous fluidity ; and that the process by which its surface became cooled resulted in the formation of a crust of granite or crystalline rocks.

2. That the surfaces of these rocks were, by the combined action of air and water, worn down and floated from higher to lower levels in running water, and deposited at the bottom of seas, lakes, &c., in layers, beds, or strata.

3. That these strata, though differing widely from each other in their composition, are respectively formed of homogeneous materials, and in an order of succession which is uniform ; that the lower members of the series are much thicker, and occupy areas of larger extent, than those above them, and especially those nearest the present surface; and that they were deposited in a position horizontal or nearly so.

4. That the entire series of stratified formations was effected by the slow and gradual operations of those

second causes, mechanical and chemical, which are at present producing analogous results; and that the process occupied inconceivable periods of duration.

5. That when by this process, and by the elevation of the deposits formed under seas, or otherwise, portions of dry land appeared, certain plants and animals were created to occupy them; and subsequently, from time to time, new creations of organic beings, terrestrial and marine, took place. That the remains of many of the plants and animals, which were created and flourished successively at different periods, were buried in the slow process by which the successive stratifications were formed, and are now discovered in a fossil state; and that the strata were subsequently upheaved by forces from below, to various degrees of inclination and elevation.

6. That the object of the stratifications, and other changes referred to, was to improve the condition of the earth, and fit it to be the abode of man.

7. That after the complement of geological changes had been effected, and the stratified series ended, the whole was thrown into a state of chaos or confusion, darkness and ruin; and was reconstructed and arranged so as to be fit for the reception of man, conformably to the account of the "six days" operations recorded by Moses. [Held by those who desire to show that their theory is consistent with the Mosaic account].

8. That in the progress of those changes, or at some period, the climate both of the northern and southern

hemisphere, and especially of the polar regions, was changed from a state of tropical heat and productiveness to a state of extreme coldness and sterility.

9. That since the date of the creation, as recorded by Moses, the same mechanical and chemical causes which operated the preceding geological changes, have been at work, but have produced but slight effects, at least within the last 3000 years.

10. That the result of the whole is, that the state of the earth is, and has been, since the date of the Mosaic creation, peculiarly fitted to be the residence, and to subserve the comfort and happiness of man.

"It is in harmony with what the Scriptures teach, to affirm that the earth as originally created was as perfect in its kind, as man or any of the creatures formed to occupy it in a state of innocence and enjoyment; perfect for the perennial and happy abode of man in his original character; perfect in the nature and combination of the materials of its surface, for the spontaneous and boundless production and support of plants and animals; perfect in all its conditions and adaptations, its temperature, its climates, its atmosphere, its freedom from everything noxious, everything tending to disease and dissolution.

"It surely will not be denied that the character of man in his primeval state, his relations to the lower animals, his physical circumstances, the career assigned to him in case of his obedience, the completeness, the harmony, the bliss of the entire scene, required a far different state of the earth, of the materials which compose its surface, of its climates, its atmosphere, and its products as to their quality, spontaniety, and abundance, from that which now exists; far different, indeed, from the conditions and adaptations, which it is in the nature of geological changes, however long-continued, to produce; far different from anything indicated in that re-construction and fitting up, and subjection to a continued and ceaseless process of change, which the geologists inform us of. That primeval epoch and condition of man assuredly implies a state of the earth which needed no improvement, no progressive course of physical changes, no geological processes to perfect its adaptations. Can any one bring himself to think that if man had not sinned and brought upon himself misery and death; that if he had continued holy, and had consequently been exempted from all evil, and confirmed in a life of perpetual innocence and blessedness, the physical conditions of the earth would be such as we find them? That any such changes, catastrophes, cataclysms, derangements, eruptions, transitions of climate, as have taken place, would have been consistent with what his well-being required? That it was at first and prior to his apostacy, more imperfect than it has been since, and therefore required to be improved by a perpetual course of geological changes?

"In short, is it not reasonable and safe to conclude,

that if the Scripture account of the creation and fall of man is to be believed; if man originally was holy and happy; if he fell from that estate, and by his fall brought death and woe into the world; the theory of the geologists as to the causes and manner of the changes which have occurred, cannot be correct.

"If there was a reason for the creation of matter and of man, a reason in the view of the Creator, who seeth the end from the beginning, and whose counsels and purposes are eternal, it doubtless embraced and had relation to, all their conditions and history. And since various, peculiar, and extraordinary Divine interpositions have undeniably attended the changes which have taken place in the moral and physical character and condition of man; why should there be such reluctance and dread to refer the changes in the condition of the earth to unusual interpositions of that power which created, upholds, and governs all? The history of man is intimately connected with that of the irrational and material world. It is scarcely bordering on the figurative to say, that when man fell, "nature through all her works gave signs of woe." This connection and joint participation in catastrophes and changes marks all their subsequent course, and the prophetic announcements indicate that the close of that course of things, in which they have been so associated, when changes in their respective condition shall be completed, will be no less signally marked by extraordinary interpositions than their creation, and the establishment of their relations originally, was. How, then, without violence to all analogy and propriety, can it be supposed that the earth, in the whole course of the changes it has undergone, was left to the operation of the *laws of nature*, any more than that all the phenomena of the moral and physical history of man should be ascribed to the operation of those laws? Can the supposition be made without virtually excluding, in both cases, all interference on the part of the Creator, after the establishment of those laws; all miracles, changes of dispensations, and, in a word, excluding revelation, and investing the laws of nature with an all-pervading efficiency?

"But what are the *laws of nature*, so familiarly referred to by our philosophers, as if they had an abstract and independent existence and efficiency, and implied something different from facts, qualities, effects, or other phenomena observed. They really mean nothing, and are nothing, more than our mode of indicating or expressing the facts, qualities, or circumstances in which the phenomena observed are perceived to agree. We call the uniformity or constancy of such agreement a *law*, as if it was the cause or reason of the phenomena. We impose upon ourselves by this high-sounding name, and by calling all that is back of it, *nature*, because we perceive nothing but the phenomena, and their coincidence or agreement. In this way the Divine efficiency may be, and often is, as truly excluded, as it would be if we should say in plain terms, that the facts, qualities, and circumstances which we observe, are their own cause.

"The rules of philosophizing restrain the geologist from supposing a preternatural cause, when he can assign any other. Hence so large a part of his attention is taken up in discovering how effects might have been produced by natural causes. There is nothing in the phenomena of Geology which would not be much better accounted for, if produced rapidly by special Divine interposition, than it can be by any gradual and ordinary operation of natural causes. And all that is wanting, in any case, is the admission of a sufficient reason for special or extraordinary interpositions. For, as such interpositions have undeniably taken place in relation to this world, both in the creation of it, and in various dispensations to man, there is nothing in the nature of the case to hinder them, or to render their recurrence improbable, whenever there was a reason.

"But let it be distinctly noted, that if the geological theory is true, then all that belongs to the moral system must be excluded from consideration in examining the physical changes in the earth. And this, in truth, is just what the philosophers hold to. For natural causes, the laws of nature are permanent and uniform, and in their ordinary operation can produce no other than ordinary natural effects. Nothing foreign to those effects could, therefore, enter into the case. Those causes might go on in one steady course, but they could work no miracles to adapt themselves, or their operations, to the exigencies of a moral system or the demands of moral causes. If those natural causes involve in their operations anything of design, it must be a design coeval with their origin and inherent in them. To talk of their being controlled and directed to any other or different end, is to talk of a miracle, as much as in the case of results contrary to, or far transcending the power of those causes. Accordingly, when the geologists speak of design, they mean the original and general design of improving the condition of the earth, and fitting it for the convenience of man. In a word, to ascribe the changes in the earth to these natural causes, is in plain terms to exclude moral causes and special reasons altogether. On the other hand, however, if those changes are due to moral and special causes or reasons; causes wholly foreign in their nature to anything incident to the laws of nature, there is nothing in those laws to hinder or interfere with the results. Those natural causes may be, as far as they go, in perfect harmony with the changes—all the mechanical and chemical agencies may be employed in producing them, though the changes themselves may be such, in their magnitude and rapidity of occurrence, as those agencies, left to themselves, would never operate.

"Now the earth presents to us indubitable evidence

of vast and manifold changes. These the geologist refers to the gradual operation of natural causes, and assigns to them the object of improving the earth. The Scriptures bring to our view moral reasons for these changes, which reasons, however, are excluded from all connection with the changes, both by the mode in which, on the geological theory, they were produced, and by their occurrence long and long before the Scripture era. Those moral reasons, therefore, are wholly shut out and at least virtually denied. They have never had any counterpart. That which they were reasons for, and which they required, has never taken place. A curse was denounced upon the earth, but it has never been executed. The earth has been improved by the Laws of Nature, but never visited for any violation of Moral Laws.

"The geologists treat the whole subject of the earth, its origin, its object, its condition and history, during the alleged incalculable periods, and down to the close of those physical changes which constitute the field of their research, just as they would if there were extant no records of inspiration; just as they would, on supposition that its creation involved no moral purposes, that it was not intended as the scene of a stupendous system of moral exhibitions, agency, and government; a scene for the trial and discipline of accountable agents, and for the most varied and wondrous manifestations on the part of their Creator; just as they would, if there had been no sin, no penal announcements or visitations, no Mediatorial interposition, no redemption achieved, or resurrection and retribution foretold.

"They begin by supposing the matter of the globe to have been somehow detached from some nebular mass, and thrust into its orbit in a state of igneous fluidity; where, becoming subject to those laws of Nature, which in accounting for physical phenomena are an unfailing resource, it necessarily assumed an oblate form. By a course of natural processes its surface at length became partially cooled and solid, and acquired a soil. At this stage of its progress, the only uses and purposes to be subserved by it, which are indicated in the whole course of the geological period, began to be disclosed by the appearance of certain vegetables and reptiles. Successive creations, growths, and inhumations, occupied myriads of ages. If there was any intelligent design, object, or purpose in this, any discoverable or probable use or intention, it was only that of giving an existence to irrational creatures, with such enjoyment as they were capable of. There were no intelligible creatures present to witness their happiness, or to observe anything of wisdom, or of goodness in their formation or condition. In all excepting their brute enjoyments, they existed for no higher purpose, and answered no higher end, than the unorganized matter around them, unless the preservation of their relics to be invoked in these last times, and made to testify against the volume of revelation, be claimed for them as a merit. They occupied, during countless ages, a mute and solitary world, which performed its ceaseless revolutions, lighted by the same sun by day, and by the same moon and stars by night, that were afterwards, when all their generations had become extinct, appointed to perform those services for man.

"Should any one, speculating on the fact that tropical plants and animals once flourished as profusely in the Arctic as in the Equatorial regions, conclude that the sun must have been created for the special purpose of furnishing the extraordinary quantity of light and heat required at the poles under those circumstances, and proceed to establish his inference by referring to the fossil remains of those regions, specifying, as to the plants, their extreme dimensions, luxuriance of growth, and other particulars, and, as to the animals, from the minutest families of indusiæ to the largest mammalia, the fact that they had eyes as well as stomachs; and should he go on to infer, that the sun, having performed this important office during countless ages, and supplied all the light and heat which were necessary during the long nights of his absence, as well as during the alternate periods of his visibility in the respective polar circles, till "the great year of geology" had elapsed, was shorn of his superfluous beams, and restricted in his office, when, for the reception and accommodation of man, the earth was reconstructed, and brought into that improved and felicitous condition which it now enjoys, with its congealed arctics, its frigid and torrid zones, and the storms, vicissitudes, and uncertainties of its temperate latitudes; he would but exemplify the spirit of that theory, which, under the intoxicating influence of novel discoveries and incomprehensible facts, and in all the affectation and pride of science, seeks to make the earth its own interpreter, disregarding or postponing all consideration of the inspired volume; he would but exhibit the spirit of that philosophy which discerns more light in the phosphorescence of a lizard's bones, than in the orb of day—more meaning in a fossil shell, than in the sacrea oracle.

"The most stupendous fact, within the cognizance of man, in the whole field of his observation and research, is the existence of that volume which discloses to us all that we know of the invisible; all that we know, or can divine, of the final causes, reasons, purposes, designs, of the creation, of the earth and its inhabitants, and of the changes they have undergone, or are yet to undergo. When regardless of this source of information, the philosopher of a fallen race, worn to a skeleton by the labor of his physical researches, and mentally subdued by the hallucination of a single idea, sets himself to account for the facts which he discovers, reasoning from an infinite variety of details to the reasons and causes of them, we need not wonder at his credulity, his presumption, his monstrous theories, his dogmatism, his intolerance, his skepticism. When he puts that volume aside for teaching what he does not like, or because he deems it too modern, too unphilosophical, or too obscure, to throw any light upon his science, he turns away from its author, fixes his gaze upon a world of creatures, unassociated with any direct or certain connection with the power or wisdom of a Creator, and plunges into the dark charnel-house of petrifactions, and the illimitable vortex of duration. Science, indeed, helps him in the discovery of facts; but, in reasoning on them, he exhibits only the blindness and imbecility of those unassisted faculties, which he employs in that process. Were he content to abstain from theorizing, from attempts to be wise in what is far beyond his sphere; content with the discovery and disclosure of facts without affecting to account for them, he would deserve respect and applause for the toil he undergoes, the patience, the self-denial, the diligence, the skill, the perseverance, evinced by his researches, and for the practical utility of his labors. But when he treats the Book of Divine revelation with contempt, and sets up his wisdom in its place, it is quite too much for him to claim or receive the sympathy and homage of any Doctors of Divinity, or other "professed friends," whose regard for that Book exceeds their ambition to be thought learned in physical science, and who would not purchase the reputation, by swallowing, blindfold, any dose prepared for them.

"A brief notice of the opinions of the geological writers, as to the inadequacy of the Noachian Deluge to account for the changes which have taken place on the surface of the earth, or any considerable portion of them, is subjoined, not with a view to suggest or support any theory of the effects of that catastrophe, as to their extent, or the mode of operation by which they were produced. The Scripture narrative is delivered in such terms as to authorize the belief that the effects of that visitation were as extensive as the object and reason of it can, to any one, appear to have required. The narrative gives it all the characters of an extraordinary visitation of Divine Providence. It was a curse upon the earth and its inhabitants. "God looked upon the earth, and behold it was corrupt: for all flesh had corrupted his way upon the earth. And God said unto Noah, the end of all flesh is come before me: for the earth is filled with violence through them: and behold, I will destroy them with the earth. And behold I, even I, do bring a flood of waters upon the earth, to destroy all flesh wherein is the breath of life, from under heaven: and everything that is in the earth shall die. And all flesh died that moved upon the earth, both of fowl and of cattle, and of beast, and of every creeping thing that creepeth upon the earth, and every man: all in whose nostrils was the breath of life, of all that was in the dry land died. And every living substance was destroyed which was upon the face of the ground, both man, and cattle, and the creeping things, and the fowl of heaven; and they were destroyed from the earth; and Noah only remained alive, and they that were with him in the ark." Immediately after the event, "The Lord said, I will not again curse the ground any more for man's sake; for [or though] the imagination of man's heart is evil from his youth; neither will I again smite any more every thing living, as I have done." And to Noah and his sons, He said, "I will establish my covenant with you; neither shall all flesh be cut off any more by the waters of a flood; neither shall there any more be a flood to destroy the earth."

"Mr. Lyell, in his brief notice of the "Supposed effects of the Flood," alludes to the opinions which had been entertained among the learned, on the question "whether the Deluge of the Scriptures was universal in reference to the whole surface of the globe, or only so with respect to that portion of it which was then inhabited by man. On the latter supposition, he thinks such an event might be accounted for by the sudden outbreak of "extensive lakes elevated above the level of the ocean," as Lake Superior is; or by the depression of large tracts of dry land below that level. He refers to volcanic and other phenomena, as indicating the improbability of the Flood having been universal; and observes, "that in the narrative of Moses there are no terms employed that indicate the impetuous rushing of the waters, either as they rose, or when they retired. On the contrary, the olive branch brought back by the Dove, seems as clear an indication to us, that the vegetation was not destroyed, as it was then to Noah, that the dry land was about to appear."

"He concludes as follows: "For my own part, I have always considered the Flood, when its universality, in the strictest sense of the term, is insisted upon, as a preternatural event far beyond the reach of philosophical inquiry, whether, as to the causes employed to produce it, or the effects most likely to result from it. At the same time, it is clear that they who are desirous of pointing out the coincidence of geological phenomena with the occurrence of such a general catastrophe, must neglect no one of the circumstances enumerated in the Mosaic history, least of all so remarkable a fact as that the olive remained standing while the waters were abating." The apparent candor of the former of these sentences is wanting in the latter. The history does not affirm that the olive remained standing till the waters were wholly withdrawn, as the sentence seems intended to imply. And it is to be observed, that Noah waited more than three months longer before he left the ark.

"The following remarks are suggested by the views of this writer.

1. He wholly omits all reference to any moral reasons for the Deluge, whether that event was local or universal, preternatural, or only the effect of natural causes.

2. He assumes that those who believe the Deluge to have been preternatural and universal, are justly to be expected to point out the coincidence of geological phenomena with such a general catastrophe. Which is as much as to say that one can have no sufficient grounds for such a belief, unless he can point out such coincidence; that the evidences of geological phenomena, that is, the inferences made therefrom, are superior to all other sources of evidence, and are to be taken as the criterion in deciding what the Scriptures teach. It might, with equal reason, be said, that he who learns from the Bible, and believes on that authority that there was a moral reason for the creation of the world out of nothing, must show how such creation could be effected, and point out the coincidence of geological phenomena with his notion of such a process; and that he who, on the authority of Scripture, believes in a resurrection, should be able to explain, "How the dead are raised up, and with what body they do come."

3. He refers to the olive leaf as the most remarkable circumstance in the narrative, against the supposition, that the flood produced any considerable effects; as though the narrative in that particular was to be taken literally, and relied on, without even an attempt at explanation, though apparently inconsistent with other parts of the history

4. His work, at large, is occupied in so accounting for the changes in the earth, as to leave nothing to be

accomplished by the flood. In accomplishing this task, however, he treats of the upheaval of mountains to account for existing phenomena, in a way, and with illustrations respecting their composition, and the existence of sedimentary deposits on their highest summits, which may well justify the supposition, that such upheaval may have occurred, for the most part, since the epoch of the Deluge, and the change of climates; and that there were no very elevated summits prior to that epoch.

"The whole time, from the day on which "all the fountains of the great deep were broken up, and the windows of heaven were opened," to the going forth from the ark, was twelve months and ten days, or 370 days. The ark rested on the 150th day; on the 223d day the tops of the mountains were seen. Forty-seven days after that, or on the 270th day, the Dove returned with an olive leaf. It was still 100 days before the earth was dry enough to permit Noah to leave the ark. Now if the flood was as long rising as falling, its subsidence commenced on the 185th day, in which case more than half the time of subsidence elapsed after the return of the Dove; if the subsidence commenced immediately after the ark rested, then nearly half the time occupied by that process passed after the return of the Dove. In either case, if the flood was preternatural and universal, and covered the tops of the highest mountains to the depth of fifteen cubits, or twenty-six and a quarter feet, then the fall during the first half of the time occupied by the subsidence can hardly be conceived to have been such as to expose any part of the general surface near the base of the mountain.

"If the tree grew on the mountain itself upon which the ark rested, midway, or at a higher or a lower point, between its summit and the level of the surrounding country, then it may well be supposed to have maintained its position, since the mountain remained, whatever changes took place elsewhere on the surface of the earth. That its position was far above the ordinary level of the country, would seem to be clearly indicated by the fact, that 100 days were required for the further subsidence of the waters; and if it occupied so elevated a position, it must of course have been upon the side or top of some mountain.

"If the olive was not situated on a primitive mountain, which remained unchanged by the deluge, but upon the ordinary soil, there was ample time, within the remaining 100 days, for its destruction, and for any imaginable extent of changes. If the leaf was plucked by the dove from a tree still standing in its natural position, probably the uppermost branches only were exposed above the surface of the water; for it was but seven days before that the dove found no rest for the sole of her foot—for the waters were on the face of the whole earth. Whatever changes in the condition of the earth the flood may have occasioned, were perhaps more likely to be effected towards the last stages of its subsidence than at an earlier period.

"It therefore does not follow, from this remarkable fact in the narrative, that the flood produced no considerable effects in the condition of the earth. Its effects, whatever they were, may, for the most part, have taken place, universally, or in particular regions, after the ark was securely seated on its resting place; and even after the plucking of the olive leaf.

"The observation of Mr. Lyell, that in the narrative of Moses there are no terms employed that indicate the impetuous rushing of the waters, either as they rose, or when they retired, is far stronger than the case will justly admit. The narrative includes such terms and phrases as the following: "I will destroy them with the earth—I will cause it to rain upon the earth forty days and forty nights, and every living substance that I have made will I destroy from off the face of the earth;—all the fountains of the great deep were broken up, and the windows of heaven were opened—and the waters prevailed and increased greatly upon the earth—and all the high hills that were under the whole heaven were covered—and the mountains were covered—and God made a wind to pass over the earth, and the waters were assuaged; the fountains also of the deep, and the windows of heaven, were stopped, and the rain from heaven was restrained; and the waters returned from the earth continually—and the Lord said, I will not again curse the ground any more for man's sake; neither shall *all flesh* be cut off any more by the waters of a flood; neither shall there any more be a flood to *destroy the earth*."

"Now, whether in so very brief a narrative of the means and operations employed in a catastrophe of a year's duration, which destroyed every thing that had life, such a statement as that all the fountains of the great deep were broken up, does not indicate vast and universal convulsions throughout the regions of the ocean, might at least be matter of question even to a geologist. If the statement was intended in any degree to account for the extent of the deluge, or to indicate the supply of waters required by the curse previously denounced upon the earth, then it is but just to consider it as indicating the most stupendous and universal action of the waters which can be conceived of; and especially, since the breaking up of all the fountains of the deep was coincident with the outpouring of such a rain during forty days and nights, as to call for the expression in the narrative, "the windows of heaven were opened."

"It is not until after the flood had attained its utmost height that we are informed that the fountains of the deep were stopped. The eruptions, or other violent action in and beneath the ocean, would seem, therefore, to have continued as long as the waters continued to rise over the land. Then, brief as the narrative is, another agent is mentioned as being introduced and employed for the sole purpose of driving the waters off from the land. "God made a wind to pass over the earth, and the waters were assuaged." The effects produced by this agent are the counterpart of those produced by the breaking up of the fountains of the deep, and may have been of like extent and violence. If the one was necessary to the raising of the waters, the other was equally necessary to assuage them. If agitation and violence attended their rising, why should they not much more attend their subsidence, since the agent employed in the latter operation is known to be capable of producing effects of that nature to any conceivable extent? And why should such an agent be specially introduced and announced, if a gradual and tranquil subsidence took place?

"But what degree of coolness must a geologist have, to contemplate such a description of a deluge, caused by the breaking up of all the fountains of the great deep, and the incessant pouring down of rain for forty days and nights, on the unequal surfaces of the earth, and perceive no likelihood of any torrents, any impetuous rushing of water, being occasioned; a geologist who can satisfy himself that the ordinary action of water, with the aid of the atmosphere, has in course of time worn down solid crystalline rocks enough to constitute the whole mass of stratifications; a geologist, who must have witnessed the effects of an ordinary rain continued for three or four days, in overflowing the channels of rivers, swelling creeks into torrents, uprooting trees, excavating the soil, and inundating the lower levels of the region; a geologist, in short, who can discern the mighty effects of small causes, if they are but natural and philosophical, but who declines all consideration of causes not in that category.

"Now, if any part of the Mosaic account of the Deluge is to be taken as meaning what it appears to mean; if that visitation was a curse previously denounced by the Creator and Moral Governor of the world; if it was executed by his own direct interposition, causing a preternatural rain of forty days, and breaking up the fountains of the deep; if the tenants of the ark were preserved, during twelve months, in their pent-up condition; if the ark itself was preserved and safely grounded on an elevation above the reach of the agitations and convulsions which attended the subsidence of the waters; if these things took place, then the same power which created the world was specially or supernaturally exerted on this occasion; the operations, to whatever extent they may appear to have been in harmony with the laws of nature, or the ordinary effects of second causes, were miraculous, and if miraculous, the magnitude of the results cannot be urged as an objection to the mode of their production. Nor can the details comprised in those operations, any more than the extent of the operations themselves, supposing them to have included all the principal changes in the crust of the globe, be urged as an objection. It is as conceivable and as credible that the materials of the sedimentary formations should, by miraculous interposition, be separated, disposed in layers or beds, and solidified in a rapid as in a gradual manner. Indeed, with respect to a large portion of the results, it can scarcely be said to be conceivable that they should ever have been produced by a slow process.

"If the Scripture narrative of the Deluge be admitted, and if it involved a miracle, then the geological theory cannot be maintained ; for that account includes a denunciation and a reason for the catastrophe, which, on the geological theory, have had no accomplishment. And here is the point where geology and the Bible are at issue. It is because the geologist assumes to account for the phenomena of the earth by ordinary second causes, to the exclusion of preternatural interpositions, and to treat the subject as though it were wholly independent of moral causes, wholly disconnected from man, and from moral government, that his speculations unavoidably conflict with the Bible, and carry him into the field of skepticism ; where, if he does not openly reject the whole of the sacred records, he rejects, or puts such construction on portions of them, as virtually to discredit and subvert the rest.

"The suggestions and arguments of Dr. Smith in opposition to the universality of the Deluge, and to the supposition of its having produced any considerable effects, are only such as might be expected from a writer under the double spell of a preconceived and favorite notion of a local and temporary submergence of a certain region in Asia, and of the theory which assigns to the changes in the earth an inconceivable antiquity ; and are deemed unworthy of any particular notice. Were his views to be taken as correct, a great deal more sagacity than they indicate would be necessary, to devise any tolerable reason why 120 years of preparation for the event was necessary, or why an Ark should have been constructed at all for the preservation of eight persons and certain animals, including the winged tribes. They might have all migrated from the scene of his local deluge, probably in three or four weeks ; and unless the Indian Ocean was raised very suddenly, and at the same time that the region to be deluged settled down, so as to pour its waters at once into the cavity, instead of requiring six months for that operation, the rest of the inhabitants and animals might have escaped as well as Noah. Moreover, if such a region settled down, and such an ocean was poured into it, what occasion could there have been to increase the supply of water by opening the windows of heaven and pouring down rain for forty days and nights ? He quite trembles at the idea that a miracle should be supposed to account for any of the facts of an universal Deluge ; and yet his own theory involves or needs ten miracles to one required by the Scripture narrative. But the whole of his views on this subject are utterly puerile, if there was anything preternatural in the Deluge itself or in any of its effects, and if there was nothing preternatural in the case, the Scripture account may as well be given up first as last. If there was a miracle, it may just as well have been a large as a small one; and doubtless was as large and as comprehensive as the occasion required. The whole matter turns upon this: was there a reason, as the Scriptures clearly intimate, for an universal Deluge? If there was, and until it can be demonstrated that there was not, it is idle, not to say impious, in man to array his petty objections to the possibility of its occurrence.

"The facts of Geology are not to be denied. That the stratified rocks, with their fossil remains, have been deposited since the creation, is past all doubts. This is the leading fact. The details comprised in it may puzzle and confound human reason and science, and occasion every variety of construction and hypothesis, without resulting in anything conclusive or satisfactory. The great question is, What was the occasion or reason of these changes? If there was a moral reason for them, then they must have taken place since the creation and fall of man. If the reason is founded in his apostacy, then so far as the Scriptures enlighten us upon the subject, it is safe to conclude that the Noachic Deluge was the means, or among the means, by which the changes were effected; and in that case there can be no more objection to our supposing a supernatural interposition to the extent required to account for the results, than there is to our believing in any miracle recorded in Scripture.

"The Scriptures tell us once, and but once, of the fountains of the great deep being broken up. Geology indicates a change in the locality of the seas. The depth of the sedimentary deposits is to the diameter of the globe as the thickness of a coat of varnish to an artificial globe. Now, with such a reason for it as the apostacy of man, it requires no great stretch of imagination to conceive that the breaking up of all the fountains of the great deep, with the other operations connected with the Deluge, the mechanical and chemical agencies, and electric and igneous forces, should have thrown all the materials of the sedimentary deposits into a state of solution and suspension in the waters, distributed those materials into homogeneous strata, diffused the fossil relics, changed the locality of the seas, and peradventure left the superficial area of ocean water several times as great as it was before. This reason, if it was a reason at all, was sufficient to occasion all the results which geology can point out.

"If the apostacy of man furnishes the reason for the physical changes which have taken place in the condition of the earth; if those changes fitted it for the abode of a fallen race; if, pursuant to the wondrous intervention for man's recovery, of Him by and for whom the earth was created, it is yet to be renovated and restored to its primitive state, and thence to be the abode only of holy and harmless beings, then is the subject cleared of all inherent and essential difficulties. Its moral requisites are satisfied, which is first and chiefly indispensable, in a matter involving the creation, character, condition and history of rational and accountable creatures, as well as the creation and condition of the earth itself, and of its irrational inhabitants. If there remain physical phenomena which science cannot explain, so there are upon the popular theory, and upon every theory. The complaint is, that science is not content to keep within its limited and appropriate province. Can science offer any explanation as to "the first introduction of a moral and intellectual being" on the earth? or as to the introduction of moral evil, by which his character and condition are, by the concession of all, so much affected? or as to the line, if there be one, which separates the purpose, province, and administration of moral government, from that which the Creator exercises over matter and irrational creatures? Upon these and innumerable other questions, connected more or less directly with the phenomena and physical condition of the earth, science is necessarily mute.

"Let it be considered that if there was such a moral reason for the changes in the earth, it is no more incumbent on those who believe that reason to be indicated in the Scriptures, to account for the mode in which the changes were effected, or to specify the instrumentalities employed, that it is to account for the creation, the fall of man, the resurrection, or any other extraordinary event or procedure in the Divine administration. We have an account of the Deluge and of the reason for that visitation, which will at least allow of the supposition of the changes in question having been produced by its instrumentality and in connection with it. It furnished the medium, water, which all allow to have been employed in those changes. If any of the phenomena attending it were supernatural, the shortness of the time of its duration, considered in relation to the magnitude of the results, can no more reasonably be urged as an objection, than the portion of time occupied in the creation can be urged as insufficient for the accomplishment of that work. It is the only event recorded in Scripture to which the changes can be assigned; and if it does not indicate the means and the occasion, we are without any historical notice of either. Here it were the part of wisdom to pause. If to the mind of a geologist objections occur founded on the phenomena which he observes; if he cannot reconcile those phenomena with the supposition that the changes took place in connection with the Deluge, whether on account of their character or extent, let him consider the intrinsic difficulties of his own theory, and the still greater difficulties which attend its bearing on Divine Revelation."

B.

The following extracts are derived from, and ought strongly to recommend the valuable work of Dr. Anderson.

"It has been no part of our vocation in these investigations to inquire into the *origin* of a material universe,—what was its pre-existent state, and by what process this globe at first was brought into an earthy, concrete form. Astronomy has tried various solutions. But whether by the splintering of other worlds, or the evolution of matter from a Saturnian ring, or the condensation of gaseous star-dust diffused through infinite space, no astronomical hypothesis has proved satisfactory. Geology is better employed when *she assumes a beginning* to her researches upon *the visible* crust of the globe. The *mystery of creation* is not within the range of her legitimate territory; and while the investigation of laws, and of the influence of secondary causes, falls within the province of both, it may be safely admitted that neither astronomy nor geology are, of themselves, capable of giving us *any real or precise account of the origin of the universe, or of any of its parts.*"—*Part* 4, *Chap.* i.

"When the geologist proceeds systematically to trace the series of these phenomena, to ascertain their causes, and to connect together all the indications of change that are found in the organic and inorganic kingdoms of nature, he attempts the structure of a THEORY OF CREATION, which shall embrace the whole course of the world, from the earliest to the present times ; and which, it may be reasonably concluded, may be resolved into one great cycle, yet unfinished. But for this the materials of the science are by no means prepared, nor is its progress sufficiently advanced."—*Ibid.*

"There are many points and questions of the deepest importance, that are far from being satisfactorily determined ;—the progress of vegetable and animal life, for example, is supposed to correspond with the varying conditions and changes of the earth's surface, when the races are summoned into existence, not at once, nor after short intervals, but successively, and after ages of unfathomable extent. The record, even as a chronicle of mere life and death, is a marvellous one, full of singular revelations, and disclosing types of organized being that have long been obliterated. But when, as yet, there was no rational head in this mundane scene, the assumption is, that the inferior tribes were for MILLIONS of years the sole living occupants of the planet! Can all the data be sound, rightly understood, and properly interpreted, that lead to such conclusions? The epic of this lengthened series of events is yet, it may be said, without a hero. The tragedy of wild revolution and carnage lacks romance in the monotony of its devastation; and destitute alike of a *moral*, and of a fitting audience, the brilliancy of the representation loses half its attractions in losing all its humanity.

"One established principle of the Science, connected with this point, is, that there are certain groups of animal species found fossil in the different sets of strata which compose the earth's crust, and that these demonstrate something like a series of distinct faunas, corresponding to the number of formations. Seven or eight sets of rocks, at least, are as distinctly characterized by particular sets of fossils. But the *exceptions* to the law are likewise very numerous, inasmuch as both species and genera have been carried forward, and *are identically the same*, from one formation and epoch into another. Hence, points, neither of difference nor of resemblance, from age to age, are absolute, and cannot very minutely be applied as regards the several formations and their organic contents. The types of one formation are repeatedly mingled with those of another; and the value of all the evidence collected from fossil remains, while it establishes undeniably a succession in *the mineral deposits*, leaves the question as to the limits of the epochs, and their relation to Time, still partially undetermined. The theory of progressive development, or that of independent acts of creation—the causes of the extinction of old and the introduction of new races—the extent of time implied or indicated in the whole series of events—and the all-important point involved in this chronology—whether all or any of the geological series are alluded to in the Mosaic account of creation,—are questions that necessarily press upon the attention, as we would solve or not the inquiries suggested. The sounding line of geology is not to be despised or cast at once aside, should it fail in furnishing a just estimate and measure of such profound investigations. Every failure will only prove a stimulus to renewed exertion, as every discovered path of error leads one step in advance towards the path of truth, and that in turn to harmony with the Book of all Truth."—*Ibid.*

[Poor consolation to a world which groaneth and travaileth in pain together until now! Poor consolation, if the truth at last to be fished up by the sounding line of geology, is of any real importance!]

" Since accurate observations are more and more multiplied, and the principles of paleontology are better understood, the doctrine of a gradual advance of animal organization toward higher and more perfect forms, as we ascend through successive deposits of the earth's crust, is daily *losing ground* among the cultivators of the Science."

"We quote the following cautionary remark of Professor Pielet :—" We ought not to be too hasty in assuming the absence of certain more perfect types in the older faunas, merely because we have not yet discovered any remains of them. We hardly know anything of these faunas, except with regard to some of the inhabitants of the sea; and it is well known that in the present condition of the globe, those animals living on land exhibit the *higher forms* of structure. Is it not possible that, in these first ages of the world, terrestrial animals also existed, more highly organized than their marine cotemporaries, although their remains *either have not been preserved, or are still to be discovered?*"—*Ibid.*, Part 4, Chap. 2.

"In the very earliest specimens of Nature's workmanship, we find the mechanism of the parts as minute, varied, and multiplied, as in those of her most recent productions. Examine the eye of the Trilobite, the oldest of the crustaceous, and the distinguishing type of the lowest of the fossiliferous rocks. These creatures swarmed in the Silurian seas. Their destiny was not fulfilled by the close of the Tertiary periods, for they *still exist.* But in none of her subsequent creations has nature displayed greater elaboration in the parts, or more skilful adaptive contrivance in their arrangements, than in the visual organ of this palæozoie family. The eye of the trilobite is formed of four hundred spherical lenses, arranged in distinct compartments on the surface of the cornea, which again projects conically upward, so as to enable the animal, while resting or seeking its food at the bottom of the waters, to take in the largest possible field of view. Fishes, birds, and mammals have all, it is well known, an optical apparatus precisely adjusted to their respective habits and the element in which they live. Fishes and fowls have their eyes differently constructed. The bat, which preys in the dark—the eagle, which soars in the blaze of the sun—and the mole, which burrows in the earth, have each peculiar and appropriate organisms. But in none is there greater complication or perfection than what is manifested in the eye of those earliest and still living tribes of the waters."—*Ibid.*

"Geology carries us back to the beginnings of organic life, when animals, each after their kind, were already perfected and endowed with a ready made apparatus for the particular sphere of existence assigned them. Every great type or class of being, whose remains are detected in the most ancient rocks of the earth, has still its representatives in living nature. The two ends of the chain, the infusorial and mammalian families, are still produced distinct, and each perfect after its kind.—"*Ibid.*, Part 4, Chap. 2.

C.

"It does not follow, because a man is eminent in geology, that his opinion is of any real value upon the *religion* of geology;—for the two subjects are quite distinct, and a man may be a Corypheus in the principles of geology, who is an ignoramus in its religious applications. Indeed, many of the *ablest writers* upon geology, take the ground that its religious bearings do not belong to the Science.

"The Theological Seminaries of our country do need, it seems to me, professorships of Natural Theology, to be filled by men who are practically familiar with the Natural Sciences. They are amply provided with instruction in the metaphysics of theology, hermeneutics, and ecclesiastical history; and I should be sorry to see these departments less amply provided for. But here is the wide field of natural theology, large enough for several professorships, which finds no place, save a nook in the chair of dogmatics. This might have answered well enough when the battle-field with scepticism lay in the region of metaphysics, or history, or biblical interpretation. *But the enemy* have, within a few years past, intrenched themselves within the dominions of natural science; and there, for a long time to come, must be the tug of war. And since they have substituted skeletons, and trees, and stones, as weapons, in the place of abstractions, so must Christians do if they would not be defeated. Although I fear that theologians are not aware of the fact, yet probably the doctrines of materialism are more widely embraced at this day than almost any other religious error. I might refer, in this connection, to the whole subject of Pantheism ; it is from biology that the pantheist derives his choicest weapons. He appeals also to Astronomy, Zoology, and Geology."—*Preface to Doct. Hitchcock's Religion of Geology.*

www.ingramcontent.com/pod-product-compliance
Lightning Source LLC
LaVergne TN
LVHW020240110826
845151LV00003B/984

* 9 7 8 1 4 2 5 5 3 0 0 2 0 *